DoMESTIC
SLUTTERY

DOMESTIC SLUTTERY

SIAN MEADES

PAVILION

CoNtEnts

LIVING 119

Introduction

Domestic Sluttery was born one rainy, winter afternoon, when I was a tad hungover and having a very bad day. I'd just lost my job, I was curled up on my sofa with a cup of tea and, despite being in a massive grump, I realized that I was in my favourite place in the world. When I think about the things that make me smile more than anything they can be narrowed down to these: good food, spending time with my friends and family and having a home that feels like mine. I launched www.DomesticSluttery.com in 2009 because I realized that those things aren't that far apart from one another. Using your favourite tea cup will make you smile as much as that plate of brownies you've just made. Sharing them with your best friends will make that smile increase ten-fold. Those things aren't exactly going to change the world, but they will make you feel good. They can turn a crappy day into a good one.

But it's not always easy to juggle a family, friends and work – and still have time for yourself. If you gave the Domestic Sluts (my colleagues and friends) a choice, laundry and dishes would be the very last thing we did. So we don't always do it (and we don't feel guilty about that either). Having sex will always be more appealing than housework. Everything is more appealing than doing housework. It's not about cleaning and cooking and having tea on the table by 5pm. Domestic Sluttery isn't about "setting up home", we're not a throwback to '50s-style femininity.

We're more realistic about our lives than that.

We might want our houses to be beautiful, but we're willing to cheat to get the lifestyle we want. We'd love to be able to cook fabulous dishes every single night, but sometimes we burn the dinner and get a takeaway instead. We're not models of perfection, but we'd like to be able to improve our lifestyle a little bit, starting with the things that we enjoy doing.

The Domestic Sluttery book isn't a self-help guide. It's not going to magically transform your life. Your life is already pretty fabulous as it is, so why not focus on that? This book looks at the most fun bits in four chapters – home, food, style and living – and it does what it can to make them a little more exciting. Instead of completely changing your life, it's about wanting to live well, saying "to hell with it" and doing the stuff that makes you happy. Whether that's booking a budget holiday to the countryside, or making brunch for your favourite people, it doesn't matter. It's entirely up to you. And no one cares if you don't bother tidying up when you're done either.

Being a Domestic Slut isn't about letting yourself go. Far from it. But there's more to life than perfection. Perfection is exhausting. Actually, it's NOT being perfect that makes women awesome. And it's finding your own brand of not perfect that makes life so much fun.

HOME SWEET HOME

"The home should be the treasure chest of living."

Le Corbusier

For the Domestic Sluts, our homes are the centre of our worlds.
Where we entertain, where we eat, where we sleep, where we
retreat. Our homes probably keep us sane. Where else are we going
to watch telly after a big night out? Or cosy up with a bottle of
wine and our best friends? Your home shouldn't be just a house.
It's more than that. It's not just somewhere you sleep and eat.

This chapter is all about making your home your own. Not turning
it into a shiny magazine page, but making it work for you. We want
you to get joy out of your house or flat, but we don't think you
need to turn your life upside down to do it. You don't need to be
an interior designer to try our tips, or millions in the bank. You
just need a little inspiration, a bit of style and perhaps a bottle of
wine or two. The rest will come together on its own. And for the
days that it doesn't, that's what the wine is for.

THE PERFECT BOUDOIR ON A BUDGET

Getting the luxurious boudoir look in the bedroom is the dream, isn't it? You want somewhere beautiful you can hide up in alone, but also a room that's equally appealing when you've got company. But getting the boudoir look on a budget? It's a little trickier, but there are simple ways to get maximum boudoir impact on minimum spends.

When you want to sleep...

Start with the bed. It's the focal point of your room and where you'll want to spend most of your time. More importantly, it's the easiest way to update your space, large or small. Buying a brand-new bed is extravagant, so stick with the soft furnishings. Cushions and comfy pillows instantly update your bed space. So does a new duvet cover. Throw in some pristine cotton sheets in as high a thread count as you can afford. Dramatic curtains and tie-backs will instantly make a room look expensive. Shut out the outside world and get some well-deserved shut-eye.

SLUTTERY TIP
Sleep is vital to your wellbeing, and a good eight hours can affect everything from your mental health to your posture. It really is worth investing in a good mattress.

When you're looking for romance...

If you're looking for something a little more decadent, try a mosquito net or canopy over your bed. It's the easiest way to make your room look fancy without making much effort. You want to create somewhere cosy but tactile. Think cashmeres, cottons, angoras and fresh linens.

SLUTTERY TIP
Think texture. Touch is
so important for creating
passion – and silks, velvets
and chiffons are all perfect
for your bedroom. There's
no such thing as "too
much", but think sensual
rather than overtly sexy.

When you want passion...

Purple is great for the sexy boudoir feel, but dark jewel colours can
be a little cold. If you can't afford a French Noir-style chandelier, get
yourself some pretty wall sconces and update your lampshades. Avoid
green lampshades – the colour of the shade might look lovely but the
light is always unflattering.

Gold is a less obvious colour to pair with purple than black. Pick up
little things that will add glam touches to the room without going
overboard. Perhaps even a little bit of gold leaf (cheaper than you'd
think in craft shops) on the skirting board. Little things like that
bring a whole room together. Fancy something really unusual? If
you're lucky enough to have wooden floorboards, go to town with
some dark lacquer. Imagine how sexy a room decorated with hot pink
furniture and black floors would be. It's not for the faint-hearted, but
then you're not faint-hearted, are you? Turn things on their head.
Once you've checked with the landlady.

Bedside table essentials

• Something to read (but nothing scary that will keep you awake). And a pretty reading lamp.
• A beautiful carafe for water when you're dehydrated in the night. Much classier than cups and glasses left all over the place. Make sure you've got painkillers for accidental hangovers too.
• Lavender essential oil: helpful for sheep-counting.
• A notebook and pen for jotting things down before shut-eye. Just make sure you don't end up working late into the night.
• Sexy things: sex toys, lube, condoms. Make sure there's a few fun things and surprises in the mix.

DOMESTIC CLUTTERY

Sexy storage solutions

The Domestic Sluts have a problem. Every single one is a magpie and attracts Way Too Much Lovely Stuff. Then there's the hoarding. Oh goodness, the hoarding. There are more shoes than anyone needs (totally necessary), enough crockery collected over the years to open a tea shop (but that would be a very pretty tea shop indeed), and favourite pieces of jewellery go missing in a flash. But gone are the teenage days when hangovers only lasted ten minutes and shoving everything under our beds was a suitable solution. That's how you end up with broken earrings and shoes that you'll never ever see again. So what is the solution to storage when most of the time it's far too much effort to tidy up?

Make it pretty

Want your storage solutions to look good? Then buy good-looking storage items. Brightly coloured boxes, shelving in interesting textures and shapes. Logic like that means you can buy more pretty things under the guise that they're essentials.

Turn everything into a display

Show off your pretty things! This is much more fun than hiding them away. Hang your prettiest dresses from hooks on your bedroom wall (it'll give you an instant boudoir feel) and display your shoes along shelves up your stairs. Display your jewellery in antique bird cages and trinket bowls.

Hide the dull

Hide anything super-boring. Keep files and papers tucked away securely. Just make sure you double check before you throw anything out – important letters sneak their way into the newspaper supplements when you're not looking.

Work the room

Start with the rooms that get the messiest. Magazines all over the coffee table? Invest in a cool magazine rack. Laundry constantly lying on the bedroom floor? Consider getting it sent out (not as expensive as it sounds – find local cleaning or laundry companies online), or buy a bigger laundry basket.

Furniture into storage

If space is really tight, buy furniture that you can turn into storage. For example, pretty ottomans with removable seat pads, or beds with underneath storage are all fantastic ways to save space. Look out for items that you can transform yourself. Furniture can be expensive, so head to the markets with some imagination and some bartering skills (see pages 152–3).

Don't apologize!

The worst thing you can do? Apologize for the mess. Yes, your house might be in a bit of a state, but people rarely notice until you point it out to them (your mother is the exception that proves this rule). Apologizing just draws attention to the fact you didn't bother tidying up before they came round. And that's always better left unsaid. Distract them with conversation and biscuits instead.

TURN YOUR HOME INTO THE TATE

You might not be able to afford your own Picasso in the loo, but each piece of artwork in your home should express your personality. Whatever your artistic style, here's how to turn your home into your very own art gallery.

Minimalist Milly

Want to display unique art but don't like clutter? Follow these steps…

PICK A WALL ANY WALL
And then absolutely go to town on it. Little prints that you like, or photos you've taken of friends and family. A mix of black and white prints will always work well. There's nothing fun about putting things in straight lines, so group prints of all sizes together. Give yourself space to have one collection and keep the rest of the walls empty for maximum impact.

ALL WHITE NOW
Art doesn't always have to mean colour. If you really want to make a statement, stick to white and go for different textures instead. Don't be tempted to paint everything white and be done with it. Without different textures your house will feel a bit like a hospital.

SINGLED OUT
Picking just one bright item in a simple room can really add impact.
Whether it's leaving a bright pink handbag on show, or a beautiful
vase of white flowers, one eye-catching piece will draw attention
without cluttering up your home.

Art Curator

If you want to play art curator, collections and clever hanging will transform your home into your own arty space.

ART IN UNEXPECTED PLACES

You never see art in the bathroom and it's rarely seen in the hallway. Try hanging a painting inside your kitchen cupboard. Little pictures here and there will make a huge difference to those left-out spaces. And they'll make you smile when you spot them unexpectedly.

DON'T LEAVE THEM HANGING

Frame pieces and leave them resting against walls in your home. This works best if you've got different-sized artworks and they're overlapping slightly. When you get bored, you can jumble them about.

POSTCARDS ARE YOUR FRIENDS

Choose ones sent by friends, or pick them up on your travels. Choose a theme and run with it throughout the house. It's inexpensive, but very effective.

Bohemian Style

Like the whole '60s art scene and hate white walls? Think patterns and personal prints on your homeware instead.

GET PERSONAL

The best thing about art is that it can be personal to you. Pick drawings that you or your kids have done and things that remind you of your friends. Or that birthday card your other half made you. You don't need to stick to framed prints. If you want to scribble all over that wall, then do it. It's your personal style that will come out, even if you did just tear out a photo from that copy of French *Vogue* you stole from the dentist.

WONDERWALL

Paint the walls different colours. It's surprising how much a lick of bright paint will make your home look like an arty studio. You don't have to stick to white walls if you don't want to (unless you rent and your landlord wants you to – always ask in advance). Paint a mural directly onto walls if you feel like it. You've got all that white space, so treat it as a canvas and play about. You can always paint over it again if you get bored.

BEYOND RETRO

Clashing and retro prints on your homewares will add splashes of colour to your home without you needing to pick up a paintbrush. Designers like Orla Kiely and Eames are a good place to start, but hunt in junk shops for real retro finds at bargain prices.

Surrealist Slut

Go crazy with your art instead of playing it safe.

HUNG UP ON YOU
Hang your art in unique ways. If you've got space, buy an easel to display your favourites. It's such a pretty way to make a feature out of artwork and you'll have a beautiful focal point. You could even hang art from the ceiling, or think about using unique frames. Make a feature of the art's surroundings as well as the piece itself.

THE CLASH
Clashing works so well in fashion, yet people shy away from it in the home. Instead of playing by the rules, mix wallpaper prints (stripes and florals work very well together), and create a striking look with pattern. The trick is not to over-do it. Keep your furniture simple, otherwise you'll look like you live in a junk shop.

SCULPT YOUR OWN STYLE
Sculpture in the home isn't easy. Instead of sculpture, get ornaments. It's sometimes a good place to start, but don't be afraid to go for something a little bigger. Seek out local art exhibitions, and smaller galleries. You'll support local artists while finding unique pieces for your home.

SLUTTERY TIP
Can't quite afford your own art work? Consider looking into Own Art (www.ownart.org.uk), who work with hundreds of designers and artists and offer interest-free loans for their pieces.

Cool Collections

If they're well-displayed, your little collections of clutter can look fantastic. Whether it's your brooch collection all grouped together, your favourite teacups or a set of vintage photographs you found in your parents' attic, they're personal to you and displaying them will add a beautiful personal flair to your home. And, if you're a hoarder, this is an easy way to convince people that you need so much stuff. It's difficult to argue when it's part of the decoration.

Think in little groups, rather than regimented and orderly. Everything all lined up doesn't look nearly as artistic (unless you want to invest in some cool shelves). Don't forget to put your pieces in unusual places. Places that don't get a lot of love in the decoration stakes are often the best place for collections.

Take your inspiration from your favourite boutiques and galleries. Look at how they display their treasures to keep them fresh and interesting and try to do the same in your house. Think simple, rather than just putting stuff on a windowsill to gather dust.

Beware of the well-meaning relative. One minute you've got a few choice pieces you love, and then suddenly you're opening your Christmas presents and every single one is a novelty teapot. Once a collection has started, it can easily get out of control.

A Few of Our Favourite Things

We love filling our homes with beautiful items, whether they're heirlooms from our Gran or something we picked up in a sale one lucky shopping day. But there are some that outshine everything else. These are the items that we'll never be parted with.

Sian: My iron coat stand. It was the first real piece of furniture I bought for myself. I picked it up in my local market for £50 and I hang everything on it – necklaces, handbags, Christmas decorations. Very rarely coats, though.

Gemma: It has to be my dressing table. I always wanted one as a kid but the closest I got was a desk that I covered in cheap cosmetics. Now I have a proper white shabby chic number ... covered in cheap cosmetics.

Frances: My "granny cabinet" that used to be my Nan's. It's glass-fronted with a pretty flower painted up the front. It's filled with lots of vintage floral teacups and is probably the most girly thing I own. Needless to say, my boyfriend hates it.

Kat: There's a core book collection that has come with me everywhere since university. Every single one has been tested for enduring awesomeness. It's my own personal library, without dust or silence. Everything from graphic novels to Jilly Cooper is there.

Alex E: I have a shocking pink chaise longue that I foolishly bought with my very first proper paycheck. I couldn't afford a TV or any other furniture, but I had my perfect pink chaise. I still love it. It's horribly uncomfortable, but I don't think I could ever part with it.

Jane: I have a collection of antique teacups and saucers that I unearthed amid an assortment of old-fashioned suitcases, records and framed photos from a grandparent's attic. They make me feel like Alice in Wonderland or Marie Antoinette – never a bad thing!

Michelle: My most treasured object is a hand-painted tile that my little girl made for me at a carnival when she was about four years old. I am planning to incorporate it into the kitchen when we redecorate. Next to it I will sit my Kitchenaid blender, which is my more materialistic favourite thing.

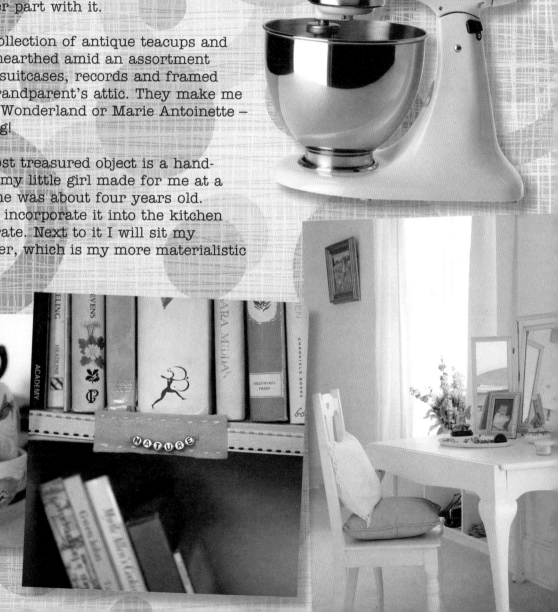

FORGOTTEN SPACES

Your living spaces are the most important in your home. You don't curl up with a book and a cuppa on the landing. But the forgotten spaces in your house or flat can undergo impressive transformations with a little bit of love.

The hallway – The first thing you see when you come in from a long day. It deserves a little bit of love for that very reason.

Your hallway will probably be the longest space in your home, so play with that. Keep it as clutter free as possible, and keep people's eyes travelling to give the illusion of more space. It's a good place for that full-length mirror. Keep the colours simple and bright and watch your space expand.

If you've got a lot of comings and goings in your house, your hallway will get messy, whether it's with junk mail and newspapers, or more pairs of shoes than you knew you had. A console table for your mail and phone, and a good coat and shoe rack are where you want to focus your decorating skills. Pop some flowers on that table too.

The downstairs loo – Lucky enough to have two bathrooms? Then it's time for a bit of fun.

If you've got a small space, play with it. Papering a whole living room with that bright patterned wallpaper you're smitten with can be excessive, but in a small space you can get away with it. So if you want flamingoes or vintage comics adorning your walls, get papering. If you can't resist that bright pink paint, grab your paintbrush. Be daring in the small spaces, and those splashes of colour and pattern will spill out into the rest of your home.

The landing – What are you supposed to do with the nothing-ey space that is the landing?

Doors are the best place to start when you're updating your landing. You can paint them a contrasting colour to the rest of the space (no, they don't need to match the room they lead into). Think a shade or two darker for the doors than the rest of the space. The area will still look bright, but you'll still get yourself a bit of colour as well. Colour is so important in your home, even if you like things minimal, colour makes us happy. Pick colours that always make you smile.

Please play with your stairs. Play with them as much as you like. Paper them, varnish them, stain them, just don't be tempted leave that ugly grey carpet covering them. Stairs should pop with colour and it's a small enough space to have a play, so do.

The utility room – The most uninspiring space in the house. Surely there's something that can be done?

This room is all about clever storage. There's really very little else that can lift a room dedicated entirely to yawnsome housework. If you've got space, consider a cupboard to hide the vacuum cleaner. Add beautiful shelving to detract from your cleaning products and line with pretty laundry baskets and decorative vintage bottles. Fill them with linen water for a cute and practical touch.

HOUSEWORK CHEATS FOR LAZY SLUTS

Any Domestic Slut would much rather be enjoying herself than doing the dishes. Alas, the chores must be done at some point (Boo! Hiss!).

As the Housework Fairy is an urban myth of Pinocchio proportions, the only option is to get creative. But don't worry, there are plenty of lazy housework cheats. They may not make housework fun – Mary Poppins isn't going to pop in with her brolly, this book isn't full of magic housework spells – but if you're short on time, don't have the right products to hand and suffer from can't-be-bothered syndrome, they're still very handy.

• A favourite trick is to hang dresses up in the bathroom while you're in the shower. It takes those creases out without even having to pick up an iron.

• Every women should have a packet of baby wipes stashed away – for wiping surfaces, mopping up spills and cleaning delicate surfaces.

• Never forget the power of white wine vinegar on stubborn stains. It gets rid of all manner of sins and mischief.

• Got a stain on a work surface that just won't budge? A black smudge on your patent shoes? Try nail polish remover. The alcohol in it will remove even the most stubborn stains. Just don't use it on anything delicate or porous.

• Cooking smells that just won't budge? Get some scented candles. Sweet smells of vanilla and cinnamon are far nicer than the smell of strong bleach spray.

• Pongy cheese? Put half a lemon in the fridge and it'll absorb all the whiffy smells. Or, eat the cheese as a mid-cleaning snack to get rid of the smell entirely.

• A dab of toothpaste on a damp cloth is good for getting grubby marks off walls, cupboard doors and light switches.

• Finally, all cleaning jobs require some kind of distraction. Have a flick through those magazines you find under the sofa. Dance about to cheesy music. It will almost make you forget that you're cleaning.

THE MORNING AFTER THE NIGHT BEFORE

Goodness, you look sleepy. Good night was it? Cup of tea to make things better? That must have been some very impressive partying. And now you have to tidy up. Hungover tidying after a party is the WORST kind of tidying. The last thing you want to do is go near anything that reminds you how many bottles of wine you got through.

You've got two choices. Either you can never go into your living room again, or you can follow these hungover tidying tips and at least make it more bearable. Don't forget our hangover tips (see pages 144–7).

Tidying Tips

#1 If you're sober enough, try to do a bit of tidying the night before. If you can clear away some bottles, glasses and beer cans, everything will look better in your hungover haze the next day. You can get stragglers to help you, too. This means less work for you or they'll finally get the hint and go home.

#2 Pick your food and drink carefully. After a mini marshmallow fight, one of the Domestic Sluts spent hours getting marshmallows out of her parents' carpet. Serve things that won't make a mess. Chocolate fondue is not your friend.

#3 Light a scented candle and open those windows. The worst thing about post-party cleaning is the smell of stale smoke and booze. Light your favourite scented candle, make a cup of tea and retire for an hour while the candle does its job.

#4 Tackle the mess in stages. Empties first. Then dishes. Then putting the furniture back where it should be. Now you're almost done! You won't eat that tiny bit of guacamole in the fridge or the crisps you left out all evening. Throw them away. Wait until the headache has gone before you attempt vacuuming.

#5 Bribe or emotionally blackmail someone else into tackling the bathroom and taking the rubbish out. This is best done with assorted brunch goodies (see pages 66–73) and cups of tea.

#6 Go and buy some flowers. Convince yourself that the bad dancing didn't happen by adding extra lovely things to the room. The walk and fresh air will help clear your fuzzy head, too.

#7 Let the hangover win. Don't even think about starting until you've taken painkillers and had more coffee. Do the worst if you can bear it, then go back to bed for a couple of hours. You'll thank us.

SLUTTERY IN THE WILDERNESS

Truth be told, the nearest most of the Domestic Sluts get to wilderness is a beer garden on a sunny afternoon, but there's no denying the helping hand that mother nature gives us in our home lives, Whether it's beautiful blooms to make a room look perfect, or a lovingly cultivated window box of herbs that help add a finishing flavour to your meal, it pays to get the most out of nature's bounty. Warning: You may have to get your hands a little dirty.

Flowers

Fresh flowers, if you look after them, will last a lot longer than you expect – but you need to keep your eye on them. A canny trick is to keep them in a clear vase so you can check their water level. If you add a packet of flower food, keep them watered and out of direct sunshine, they'll last for ages – sometimes for as long as two weeks.

SLUTTERY TIP
Sweet peas in summertime smell so good. If you spot some, buy them!

So what else do you need to consider when you're buying fresh flowers?

• Pick pretty colours! This is the best bit about buying flowers. You can choose them just because you like the colour. Actually, that's probably the only reason you need to have. Be wary of buying lilies if you've got cats – they might be beautiful but their pollen is poisonous to our curious furry friends and not all of them are clever enough not to have a sniff.

• Cut off excess leaves. Any leaves and stems that will be in the vase are just stopping water getting to the flowers, meaning your blooms won't last as long.

• Don't stress if you break one. It happens! They're fragile. Especially if you're carrying them home on a crowded bus.

• Buy in season. Not only are flowers prettier in season, but they're better value, and always last longer. What could be better than a bunch of daffs or sunflowers when they're coming into bloom?

Classy container cultivation

The other way to introduce a bit of plant life into your home life is to grow your own. If space and time are limited, it's time to get creative. There's a lot you can grow in a simple window box while, for those with backyards, a bit of clever container planting can produce more than you'd think. It makes the space look a lot prettier, and does wonders for personal wellbeing, too. Scrubbing the soil off a home-grown carrot is so much more satisfying than tearing open some plastic wrapping from the supermarket. It's really easy to get overwhelmed by the huge amount of information on gardening that's out there, so try to keep it simple at first, enjoy a bit of experimentation and see what happens. Remember, plants want to grow – it's what they were made to do. Just give them a helping hand and then they'll do what comes naturally.

SPACED OUT

First of all, think about the space you have available. Room for a few tubs and grow bags? That should be enough to give you a good harvest of potatoes and carrots. Just space for a window box? That's more than enough for a good crop of useful herbs. Different plants need different amounts of space and soil to grow in. For example, onions and root veg need a soil depth of about 30–45cm (11¾–17¾in) to grow, while you can get away with a lot less for herbs and salad seeds. Many plants come in dwarf varieties especially for those with limited space. Planning and calculations done, most important of all is remember to plant what you actually use and enjoying eating!

SOWING YOUR SEEDS

You need to decide on a suitable home for your precious seeds. You can buy ready-made containers, but think like a Domestic Slut and go for re-use. Take the labels off olive oil or tomato tins and you've got a contemporary looking container without spending any cash. Wooden crates, a sink that's been liberated from a skip – there's loads of imaginative solutions. Whatever you use, remember to add holes in the bottom of the container for drainage. Invest in one of the special washes that are available to clean out your container and make sure there are no evil plant-eating bugs lurking inside.

Whatever space you have, think about giving your plants the best possible opportunity for growth. That means plenty of sunshine and water. Place your box or tubs in the bit of outdoor space that gets the most rays possible. If you're using a window sill, remember that it probably will be a bit sheltered from the rain, and you'll need to keep watering it yourself. Keep a tub outside to collect rainwater – much more favourable to plant growth than the treated water that comes out of the tap.

You'll need to add a layer of stones to the bottom of your container to help with drainage before adding your compost and then you're ready to plant. Read the back of your packets of seeds. Too many good intentions have been ruined by packing too many seeds too close together and planting in the wrong place. If you don't want to bother working out the proper distance between plants, you can even buy seeds on strips that have worked all that out for you and are simply ready to be planted.

If you've got a bit more space outside, it's worth looking at grow bags. They work well for salad leaves, but you can stack them up to add depth to your soil and try out things like aubergines and chillies.

WONDERWALL

Have a wall you can use? You're lucky if it's south-facing for maximum sunshine and you can grow upwards. Garden centres sell vine hooks that will help runner plants grow up your wall. Squashes are quite good for this. Remember, you could also have a go at attaching some of your containers to the wall too – just make sure they're properly attached. Nobody likes a squashed tomato!

Once you've got your garden growing and you've begun harvesting the fruits of your labour, you'll get more used to the different planting cycles of your vegetables, as well as their yield – the volume of courgettes produced by one innocent looking plant can be overwhelming! Keep an eye out for the herbs that don't naturally regrow – coriander and cress are prime examples of these. Start growing fresh batches in yoghurt pots inside your house, ready to transfer to your window box or container once the current supply is used up. That way, you should never need rely on the supermarket salad selection again.

Alas, you and your nearest and dearest won't be the only ones who find your harvest a tasty proposition. Which brings us to a fearsome topic …

The beastly world of bugs and butterflies

If you're lucky enough to have some proper outdoor space, you need to work out which bugs will help your garden grow and which will make it groan. Watch the cinematic classic 'A Bug's Life' and you'll realize that all creatures (great and small) have their place in their ecosystem, no matter how creepy or crawly they are. However, there's no denying that some creatures happen to be cuter and more useful than others.

Here's the Domestic Sluttery guide to navigating this critter-cal terrain.

SHOO FLY, DON'T BOTHER ME – THE ONES YOU DON'T WANT HANGING AROUND:

Slugs: Fat and ugly and slimy and destined to destroy your prettiest blooms. Make a slug pub – a plastic tray full of beer designed to entice the slugs to take a dip. They die drunk and happy and your plants will live to see another day.

Aphids: Also the devil incarnate when you're trying to make your garden grow. Chives, onion and garlic not only scare away potential snogging partners but do the job for aphids, too. Or you could introduce them to a few ladybirds.

Spiders: Spiders are pretty harmless, they just ain't pretty. Nothing that has eight eyes is pretty. The essential oil citronella should help, or call up the heroic ladybird if they really pester you.

Moths: Not so much a problem outside, but get them in the house and they are sure to make a meal of a cherished jumper. Natural remedies to keep them away include lavender and sandalwood.

SIMPLY THE BEAST – THE ONES TO BEFRIEND

Ladybirds: These are not only the best-dressed insect around (loving the polka dots, ladies) but are one of the most helpful, too. They help you say adieu to aphids and so long to spindly spiders, you can repay the favour by making them a nice place to shelter and survive. Try planting ferns and evening primroses.

Beetles: All you need are ground beetles if you want to say goodbye to creatures like aphids, leatherjackets, slugs and snails. You can encourage ground beetles by providing them with nice damp log pile to shelter in.

Centipedes: A dose of lethal venom from brown centipedes knocks out slugs and vine (evil) weevils.

Worms: They should worm their way into your affection, being brilliant at breaking down the dead material and mixing it together in the soil. It's simple to make or buy a worktop wormery to break down any leftover kitchen waste – it makes for an especially fruity fertilizer and will help all the plants in your lovingly planted window boxes and containers grow.

Bees: Our buzzy little friends do more than you might realize. They pollinate our food and flowers (and make tasty honey), so they need looking after. What flowers will have them making a bee line? They especially like tube-shaped flowers, so foxgloves and wonderful snapdragons will soon turn your garden into a hive of activity.

Butterflies: They don't help your garden to grow any better, but they certainly make it look pretty. They like nectar-rich herbs and wildflowers. Sow bluebells and primroses for spring as they emerge sleepy and hungry from hibernation. Fatten them up for autumn with forget-me-nots, honeysuckle, lavender, mint and thyme. Tortoiseshell and Peacock butterflies also enjoy a good old feed on nettles. Indulge their strange food habits and you'll reap the rewards on a summer's day as you sit outside, drink in hand, with beautiful butterflies fluttering around you.

Food and Drink

"One of the very nicest things about life is the way we must regularly stop whatever it is we are doing and devote our attention to eating."

Luciano Pavarotti

The Domestic Sluts are always thinking about food. Sometimes it's about stealing ten minutes by yourself for a biscuit and a cuppa, sometimes it's a gourmet meal. But it should always be about enjoying what you eat.

We're not going to tell you how to decorate a six-tier wedding cake. And we won't show you how to create a five-course meal for twelve without breaking into a sweat. Instead, we will share some of our favourite recipes. The ones that we make time and again because just the smell of them makes us instantly happy.

Cooking shouldn't be about chaining yourself to your hob. For us, it's about have a play with whatever is in the fridge, trying to recreate that tasty chicken thing we had in our favourite restaurant, and realizing that it's OK you incinerated the biscuits. Again. They're just biscuits. We want people to enjoy food. For us, that starts right at the beginning. The best ingredients we can afford, a little imagination, and a love of eating and sharing tasty things with people we really like.

Sluttishly Simple

Sian says... Simple cooking doesn't mean bland and tasteless. When it's done well, it means you've got good ingredients and you know how to use them. It means that you'll always be able to knock something up from contents in your fridge, and you won't be reaching for the takeaway menu.

DIY curry

Indian cuisine doesn't have to mean hours in the kitchen. Plenty of curry recipes follow the same basic steps, and once you've mastered those, you can experiment with whatever ingredients you fancy. This easy curry recipe will teach you the basics.

SLUTTERY TIP
Keep your spices in an airtight container, away from direct sunlight. Sunlight will sap those strong flavours.

Make it!
• Heat the oil over a medium heat. Add the mustard seeds. When they start popping, add the cumin seeds. Don't burn them – they'll taste horrid.
• Fry the garlic, onion, ginger and chopped chilli for around 10 minutes, or until the onion is soft. Add the remaining spices and stir for a minute. (Add extra ground chilli if you like it fiery.) If you're making a meat dish, chop 400g/14oz of your meat into bite-sized pieces, and brown it in the pan.
• Now add the basis of your sauce. Chopped tomatoes are ideal, or you may prefer coconut milk for a milder taste. If you're making a pescetarian or veggie curry, now is the time to add your fish, beans or veg of choice. Chop fish into bite-sized pieces and simmer gently in the sauce for 8–10 minutes until it flakes easily. If you're using pulses or vegetables, mix in and simmer for 15–20 minutes until soft.
• Season to taste, stir in some garam masala, sprinkle with chopped coriander leaves and serve immediately with rice or naan.

Serves 2

You will need:

2 tbsp olive oil
1 tsp mustard seeds
1 tsp cumin seeds
1 garlic clove, crushed
1 onion, finely chopped
5cm/2in ginger, grated
1 chilli, finely chopped
½ tsp turmeric
1 tsp ground coriander
½ tsp ground chilli
400g/14oz meat, fish, beans or
veg of choice
400g/14oz tin of chopped
tomatoes or a tin of
coconut milk
2 tsp garam masala
small handful of coriander
leaves, chopped

Chicken and chorizo paella

Traditional paella is loaded with beautiful fresh seafood. This version was created for someone with a shellfish allergy, so contains none, but you can add whatever fresh seafood you want. Saffron is used to give the rice the characteristic yellow colour, and it really does make this dish more authentic. However, since saffron costs more than gold, you can omit it if you're on a budget – the chorizo oils add an orange sheen and a gorgeous smoky flavour.

Make it!

• In the widest pan you can find, heat the olive oil and add the garlic, pepper and onion. Sauté for 5–10 minutes until the peppers are soft and the onions translucent. Set aside.
• Add the chorizo to the pan and fry until the oils start to come out. Add the chicken and fry for another 5 minutes or so until cooked through. Add the rice and all the herbs and spices except the saffron, and stir until the rice is coated in the juices. You may need to add more olive oil – your rice should look nice and glossy.
• Pour in most of the stock, reserving 50ml/1¾fl oz/¼ cup. Add the saffron, onion, pepper and tomatoes and quickly stir through to make sure all the ingredients are covered. Bring to a simmer and leave to bubble away without touching. The key with paella is to avoid stirring so you get separated, not creamy, rice.
• When the liquid is three-quarters reduced (15–20 minutes), taste the rice. You want a melting texture. If you think it needs longer, add the rest of the stock (and extra water if needed). Leave again without stirring until all the liquid has been soaked up and the veggies are cooked but still have a bit of life in them. The peppers will have all but disappeared, but that's fine – the flavour remains. If the rice has started to stick to the pan, don't worry. That's actually the tastiest bit. You can even turn up the heat a little at this point to burn off the last of the liquid and get that much-loved "crust". Turn off the heat and allow the paella to sit for a couple of minutes before serving.

Serves 4

You will need:

2 tbsp olive oil
4 cloves garlic (crushed) or
1–2 tsp garlic purée
2 red peppers, cut into chunks
2 onions, roughly chopped
125g/4½oz chorizo sausage,
sliced thinly or cut into
small chunks
6 chicken thigh fillets or
3 large chicken breasts
250g/9oz/1¼ cups paella rice
2 tsp paprika
1 tsp chicken seasoning mix
1 tsp dried thyme
1 tsp dried oregano
500ml/17½fl oz/2 cups chicken
stock
a few strands of saffron,
soaked in an egg cup of
hot water
3 ripe tomatoes, seeds
removed, diced

Chilli prawn pasta

Pasta is the Domestic Slut's secret weapon. After a bad day at work, it'll cheer you up and make you forget that you accidentally deleted the document you'd be working on all week. When you get in late, you can make it in minutes. And when you've forgotten you have friends coming over for dinner, it'll save you from having to get a takeaway.

This prawn pasta has a strong chilli kick, and the marinade doubles as a subtle sauce for the pasta itself. It takes just 15 minutes, so even when you're at your busiest, you've still got time for a tasty home-cooked meal.

Serves 4

You will need:

500g/18oz prawns
juice of 1 lime
1½ tbsp olive oil
dash of light soy sauce
dash of fish sauce
1 red and 1 green chilli,
finely chopped
2 cloves garlic, crushed
300g/10½oz pasta (long-strand
pasta like tagliatelle or pappardelle
will work best)

Make it!

• Put the prawns in a dish with the liquid ingredients and garlic and chilli. Mix well and leave to marinade while you get the pasta on. Prawns pick up flavour quickly, so they don't need to marinade for hours.
• Pop the pasta on to boil in a large pan.
• Once the pasta is al dente, strain and set to one side. Transfer the prawn mixture to the pan (no need to add extra oil), and simmer slowly for a few minutes.
• When warmed through, begin adding the pasta back to the pan in batches. Adding the pasta gradually means that you can get all of those strands coated in the yummy sauce and all the prawns will mix in without your pasta turning into a massive gloop.
• You're done! Place in a large bowl in the middle of a table, let everyone help themselves and fight for the last serving. Serve with salad, white wine and lots of laughter.

Enough for a large loaf, 8 bread
rolls, or 3 large pizza bases

You will need:

500g/17½oz/4½ cups strong white
bread flour
1 tsp salt
7g/¼oz sachet of fast-acting yeast
(approx 1 tbsp)
2 tbsp olive oil
300ml/10½fl oz/1¼ cups
lukewarm water

Basic bread dough

Nothing compares to the simple pleasure of taking
a home-baked loaf out of the oven. Once you realize
how easy it is to make your own dough, you'll be
whipping up your own rolls, loaves and pizza bases in
no time. Kneading the dough is therapeutic and stress-
relieving, and casually mentioning to friends that, by
the way, you made that bread, is priceless. Use this as
a basic guide and get experimenting. Add olives, dried
tomatoes or herbs to the dough, plait it, sprinkle poppy
or sesame seeds over the top – try whatever you fancy.

Make it!

- Sift the flour and salt into a large bowl and add the sachet of yeast. Drizzle the olive oil over it and roughly mix it through.
- Make a well in the middle and gradually add the water. Use a fork to bring the flour in from the sides and mix it into the water, bringing in larger and larger amounts until it starts to come together. Using a fork rather than your hands keeps the dough nice and loose.
- When it starts to come together, work the rest of the flour in with your hands until it forms a loose ball. Tip it out onto a floured surface and get kneading.
- This is the stress-relieving part. Roll it, pull it, flip it and bang that dough down on the countertop. The best method is to hold the dough down with one hand and stretch it away from you with the other. Fold it back towards you, swivel the dough 90 degrees and repeat. Notice how it changes texture as you knead, becoming silky and elastic after about 10 minutes. You'll be able to stretch it further and further without it breaking, and it will spring back when you push your fingertip into it.
- Put the dough into a large bowl and cover the top with a clean tea towel. Leave it in a warm room until it has doubled in size, which takes about 60–90 minutes. If you don't have anywhere warm to leave it, then turn your oven onto its lowest setting for 5 minutes, turn it off, and pop the covered bowl in there. (Alternatively, leave it to rise slowly in the fridge overnight. The cold temperature won't harm the yeast and will produce a loaf with a moister texture.) Be patient – the yeast needs to feed off the natural sugars in the flour and produce carbon dioxide. This creates bubbles in the dough, making it rise. When the dough has risen enough, punch it down to knock the air out, and shape it into a large loaf, pizza bases or rolls. Transfer onto a lightly oiled baking tray, cover with a tea towel and let them rise for another 10 minutes. Preheat the oven to 220°C/425°F/Gas Mark 7.
- For loaves or rolls, lightly brush them with a beaten egg or milk and bake for 25–35 minutes, depending on their size. (For pizza bases, see our tips on page 51.) To check they're done, turn them over and tap them on the bottom. If they sound hollow, they're done. Leave to cool on a wire rack before devouring.

SLUTTERY TIP
Dough too dense? Add half a teaspoon of sugar. Making wholemeal bread? Counteract its heavy texture by crushing half a 500mg vitamin C tablet and adding it to the dough. It will yield a much lighter loaf.

Post-work pizza

If the thought of a supermarket pizza – covered in plastic cheese and pathetic-looking toppings – is too dispiriting, then make your own from scratch. This dough recipe makes a wonderful pizza base and it's quick enough to whip up when you get in from work. Top with homemade sauce and your choice of toppings for a pizza that's delicious when you've got the evening to yourself, but even better when accompanied by friends, cocktails and salacious gossip. This will give you enough for 3 large pizzas. The bases will look thin, but remember they'll puff up in the oven.

Make it!

- Prepare the dough for the base (see page 48).
- While it's doing its thing, get on with your sauce. Fry the garlic in the oil over a medium heat for 10 seconds, then chuck in the tomatoes. Add the wine, sugar, oregano, chilli flakes and seasoning. Simmer the tomatoes whole for around 10 minutes. If you break them up too early, you'll end up with a sauce made bitter by the tomato seeds. When they're falling apart and the sauce is thickening, after about 20–25 minutes, blitz it all with a blender. Add some torn-up basil leaves and you're done.
- Shape your pizza base and prepare your toppings. Fry or grill any meat, chop the veg, grate your cheese.
- Heat the oven to 220°C/425°F/Gas Mark 7. Add your tomato sauce and toppings to the base. Resist the temptation to overload it, or it'll be soggy in the middle. Bake for 8 minutes on the tray, then slide it off to cook for a further 5–8 minutes directly on the oven shelf. This will crisp-up the base.
- It's a shame to waste the rest of that wine, so pour a glass, curl up on the sofa, and tell yourself you'll keep half the pizza for tomorrow. Then accidentally eat it all.

You will need:

For the base:

see standard dough recipe (page 48)

For the tomato sauce:

1 tbsp olive oil
1 garlic clove, chopped
450g/16oz tin of whole plum tomatoes
100ml/3½fl oz/½ cup red wine
1 tsp sugar
2 tsp dried oregano
½ tsp chilli flakes
fresh basil leaves, torn
salt and pepper

Topping ideas:

peppers, onion, cherry tomatoes, mushrooms, olives, ham, chorizo, bacon, chicken, turkey, tuna, anchovies, mozzarella cheese

Serves 4

You will need:

4 eggs
120g/4oz/1 cup plain flour
200ml/7fl oz/1 cup milk
salt and pepper
1 tsp dried thyme
vegetable oil
6 sausages

Toad in the hole

Toad in the hole is the perfect, quick, carb-filled dinner. Use meat or vegetarian sausages and add your favourite herbs to the batter.

Make it!
• Preheat the oven to 220°C/425°F/Gas Mark 7.
• Make the batter first. Tip the flour, seasoning and thyme into a bowl, make a well in the middle and add the eggs. Beat together and slowly add the milk until the mixture resembles single cream. Leave in the fridge while you sort out the sausages.
• Use a large roasting tin and cook 6 whole sausages in 2 tablespoons of hot oil for 15 minutes. Pour the batter over the top. Cook for 35–40 minutes, then serve.

Fancy a smaller snack? Use a muffin tray instead.

• Put 1 tsp of oil in each cup of the muffin tray and heat in the oven for 5 minutes until the oil is smoking hot. Put two pieces of sausage into each cup and bake for 15 minutes until browned.
• Remove the tray and pour the batter into each cup until two-thirds full. Bake for 20–25 minutes, until beautifully risen and golden brown.

Cooking Disasters

Think the Domestic Sluts are all mini
Delias in the kitchen? Think again. We
have accidents, we ruin our dinner and
we've almost been guilty of a few fires.
Feel bad about burning your biscuit
bottoms? Here are some of our biggest
culinary disasters.

Sian: I nearly burnt down the Home Economics room at school. I wasn't paying attention when my teacher was explaining the most complicated microwave IN THE WORLD. My chocolate burnt, the microwave had smoke pouring out of it and I was left with a telling off and no chocolate mousse to take home.

Instead of using a microwave to melt chocolate (you've got no control over the speed), use a bain-marie. Just pop a Pyrex bowl over a pan of simmering water and melt away.

Kat: Other than cooking when drunk, which is a bad plan unless your guests are steaming as well, the worst thing I've ever done is not scrub or peel potatoes (I know, I KNOW!) A few years ago I made a lovely shepherd's pie, looked at the potatoes and decided to skip it. The entire golden mash topping tasted of purest soil.

Ladies! Those steps are there for a reason. Don't go skipping them.

Sara: Grilling some fairy cakes during Home Economics at school. Nothing could have saved them, other than a time machine and a working knowledge of what the dials on the oven meant.

Stuff like this happens more than the Domestic Sluts care to admit. Instead, pop to the shop and buy some biscuits.

Alex E: I have had lots of disasters, but probably the most memorable was when I forgot the eggs in a cake. My WEDDING cake. The cake was all flat and greasy, and I couldn't work out what I'd done wrong until I saw the eggs I had counted out on the worktop. Luckily I had time to make it again before the big day!

Always check the method. And if you're doing something for a special occasion, leave enough time for disasters to happen. Because they do.

Veggie, not Virtuous

Sara says... I became a vegetarian pioneer when, aged 8, I announced I was no longer eating meat. This was no principled stance, I was just an incredibly picky eater. I lived on potato waffles for the next decade. More than 20 years later, I've branched out and found plenty of vegetarian food that I adore and I've never missed meat. These recipes show that you don't have to sacrifice flavour or texture when you cut out meat.

Halloumi on a bed of spicy lentils

If you miss the texture of meat, then halloumi is your new best friend. Try it in a fried breakfast instead of bacon. It's salty, tangy, and dangerously moreish.

Peppery puy lentils don't disintegrate when you boil them, so add a more interesting texture than traditional lentils.

Make it!

• Boil the dried lentils in unsalted water for 15–20 minutes until slightly al dente. Drain, then return to the saucepan. If you're using tinned lentils, just gently heat them through.
• Heat the oil in a small frying pan over a medium heat and fry the onion, garlic, chilli and cumin until the onions are soft. Tip them into the lentils, and pop the lid on to keep warm.
• Fry the halloumi for 1–2 minutes on each side over a medium-high heat until golden brown in parts. Grill it for the same time if you prefer. For a spicier kick, sprinkle with a little chilli powder before cooking.
• Arrange the halloumi on top on the lentils and eat it hot for dinner. Add some cherry tomatoes and a squeeze of lemon juice to any leftovers and eat as a cold lunch the next day.

Serves 2

You will need:

150g/5¼oz dried puy lentils, rinsed and drained; or a tin of puy lentils, drained
300ml/10½fl oz/1¼ cups water
small red onion, sliced
2 cloves of garlic, crushed
1 tbsp vegetable oil
½ tsp ground chilli powder
½ tsp ground cumin
250g/9oz pack of halloumi, cut into 1cm/⅜in thick pieces, or thinner if you like

Veggie burgers

Veggie burgers veer from nicely spiced patties that are visibly full of vegetables to spongy rounds of mush that disintegrate as soon as you bite into them. Let us not even speak of meat-replacement burgers – those thin joyless slabs of greying cardboard that have to be covered in ketchup to give them flavour.

Makes 6

You will need:

2 tbsp vegetable oil
2 tsp cumin seeds
2 onions, diced
2 garlic cloves, crushed
2 tsp ground coriander
2 x 400g/14oz tins of kidney beans, rinsed and drained
100g/3½oz/1 cup plain flour
1 tsp dried rosemary
2 tsp chipotle paste

Instead of playing supermarket roulette and hoping you find a decent batch, why not make your own at home? They're suspiciously quick and easy to do, and they can be cooked straight from the freezer, making them ideal if you're in a hurry or trying to avoid the kebab shop on the way back from the pub.

Chipotle paste is made from smoke-dried jalapeño peppers, onion and tomato, and adds a rich smoky warmth to the burgers. You'll find it in the Mexican foods aisle, next to the fajita kits and salsas. You can substitute some chilli powder if you can't track it down.

Make it!

• Fry the cumin seeds in the oil over a medium heat until they start to pop. Add the onion and garlic and fry for around 5–6 minutes. When the onion softens, add the ground coriander and fry for another half a minute.
• Tip the kidney beans into a bowl and mash them with a potato masher. Don't use a food processor unless you want your burgers to have a weirdly uniform texture. For variety, try a combination of kidney beans, black beans or chickpeas. Add the cooked onion and garlic, chipotle paste, dried rosemary, flour and seasoning.
• Wet your hands and form the mixture into six patties. You can freeze them now if you like. To cook them, dust with a little extra flour (or coat in breadcrumbs for a crispy outer coating) and either shallow-fry them or grill them on a non-stick tray for 4 minutes on each side. If you're cooking them from frozen, stick them in the oven at 200°C/400°F/Gas Mark 6 for 25 minutes.
• And that's it – you're done. This really is fast food. You should be in and out of the kitchen in less than half an hour. Serve in a floury bun with salad and ketchup.

Store Cupboard Essentials

There is nothing more miserable than an empty kitchen. Your kitchen should be vibrant and full of ingredients that you love, from healthy wholegrains to indulgent sweet treats. Store cupboard essentials are the ingredients that form the basis of most home-cooked meals, the ones you should replace without thinking about it. You'll save money in the long run, as there'll be no more evenings where you stare hopelessly into the fridge, wondering if you could have gin and biscuits for dinner, before shrugging your shoulders and reaching for a takeaway menu.

Cupboards

Oils

- Neutral oil – such as vegetable or sunflower for frying
- Olive oil – for general cooking or drizzling over salads
- Sesame oil – for stir-fries and other Asian cookery

Basic carbs – to form the basis of any meal

- Dried cous-cous
- Noodles
- Pasta
- Potatoes
- Rice

Vegetables

• Onions and garlic will keep for ages in a cool, dark place

Basic baking

• Baking powder – add to plain flour to make self-raising flour
• Caster sugar – the basis of all sweet treats is fine sugar, not the stuff you put in your tea
• Plain flour – for general baking and cooking
• Strong white flour – use this for bread
• Vanilla extract – not flavouring
• Yeast sachets

Herbs and spices

• Basic Indian spices – cumin, coriander, chilli, turmeric, garam masala
• Bay leaves – they add depth and flavour to chicken and stews
• Cinnamon – with baked apples or cakes
• Mint – for lamb dishes and cous-cous
• Oregano – for Italian and tomato dishes
• Paprika – with roast pork, homemade hummous or scrambled eggs; try smoked paprika if you want to add a rich smokiness to your dish
• Sage – use sparingly with pork, chicken, beef or pasta dishes
• Salt and pepper
• Stock cubes – great for kickstarting a sauce or stew
• Tarragon – with French cuisine, eggs or chicken
• Thyme – for tasty chicken and marinades

Tins

- Chickpeas – roast them with spices for a tangy snack, blitz into hummous, or tip into a vegetable madras
- Chopped tomatoes – add to a chilli, curry or baked-potato topping
- Kidney beans – bulk out a stew or chilli
- Tuna – in a sandwich or on a baked potato
- Soup – not just for lunch, but also as a speedy pie filling
- Whole tomatoes – for simmering down into a pasta sauce

Alcohol

- One bottle of red wine and another of white wine – not only handy for unexpected guests, but also great in sauces
- Vodka, gin, whiskey, amaretto … your spirit of choice, just because

Fridge

- Butter – no Domestic Slut is ever without butter
- Cheese – a block of Cheddar and packet of halloumi for starters
- Chocolate – there's nothing nicer than dark chocolate straight from the fridge (to grate over dessert or cram into your sobbing face because it's Day 27)
- Eggs – whip up everything from a brunch to a cake
- Lemons – squeeze over fish and salad, into sauces, or slice into a gin and tonic
- Milk – if you can't make a cuppa, you're done for
- Tomato purée – adds oomph to sauces and dishes looking a bit pale and bland

Freezer

- Chicken breasts – just make sure you defrost properly before cooking
- Fish – especially fish fingers for sandwiches
- Frozen veg – boil them to accompany a meal, throw them into a curry, make an impromptu stir-fry. Frozen vegetables keep their nutrients, but won't have the texture or flavour of fresh ones
- Mince – beef or soya
- Peas – they'll bulk out any meal, not to mention sort out a twisted ankle
- Pitta – emergency carbs to go with a curry, or to stuff with a cous-cous salad
- Frozen chips – when it's just too much effort to peel, chop and roast some spuds
- Puff pastry – for chicken pie or salmon en croute
- Stock – simmer up any roast chicken bones with some root veg for a few hours, strain and then freeze
- Sausages – such a comforting staple

The Perfect Hamper

Want to give good grub? One of the best foodie gifts to put together is a hamper full of tasty delights. You can tailor it to the tastes of the lucky recipient and to your own culinary talents. The centrepiece of this hamper is a tender and gooey ham; add in a few gourmet extras and you've got a gift that keeps on giving delicious foodie love.

SLUTTERY TIP
Giving festive gifts? Jazz up your hamper with some homemade mulled wine spices. Make up a mix of nutmeg, cloves, ginger, cardamom and cinnamon sticks and wrap in a little bouquet garni bag (or square of muslin).

You've put the ham into the hamper, so how do you add the perfection? Think of treaty trimmings. It's time to relish your relishes. English mustard, apple chutney and piccalilli would all be perfect partners to the ham. Pickled walnuts or beetroot are nice savoury additions for a hamper, but there's nothing like a good ol' pickled onion on your paper plate.

Maple and marmalade roasted ham

Pork is the most versatile meat. Ideally, all meals would involve pork. Brunch would be nothing without bacon (see page 71), and chorizo is a pig staple. Pork goods make most Domestic Sluts giddy with their enticing cooking smells and we're powerless before them. But there's one porkstuff that's often overlooked because people think it's a pain the backside: the ham. Glistening with syrup and tender and tasty whether it's hot or cold. It'll work for every pork-based occasion you might have. Sunny picnics, snoozy and boozy Boxing Days, or even just a late-night-standing-at-the-fridge snack.

Make it!

- Place the gammon in the largest saucepan you have and cover with water. Add the carrot, onion, leeks and celery. Throw in the peppercorns and bay leaves and leave simmering on a low heat for 2½ hours (go read a book). Top up with water if needed (you can use this stock in soup, so make sure you strain and freeze it); but don't cook for any longer – the veg will turn to mush and make your little piggy taste horrid.
- Preheat the oven to 190°C/375°F/Gas Mark 5. Remove the gammon from the water and let it cool for 15 minutes. Score the skin in criss-crosses and add the cloves at the intersections.
- Mix the syrup, sugar and marmalade on a low heat until melted. Place the ham in a roasting tin and pour half the glaze over the top of the ham, ensuring that the top and sides are coated. Roast for 30 minutes, or until the glaze has browned. Make sure you turn 3–4 times while baking, adding more glaze where necessary, so it's all evenly golden.
- When cooked, transfer to a wire rack that has a plate underneath and allow to cool for 15 minutes before serving. Carve into slices and serve hot with chutney, or cold in yummy sandwiches with some strong cheddar and mustard.

Serves 6

You will need:

For the ham:

1kg/2¼lb unsmoked gammon joint
1 carrot, chopped
1 onion, chopped
2 sticks of celery, chopped
1 leek, chopped
handful of peppercorns
2 bay leaves
cloves, for studding

For the glaze:

40ml/1½ fl oz/3 tbsp maple syrup
1 tsp sugar
1 tbsp marmalade

Brilliant Brunch – the best meal of the day

Breakfast might be the most important meal of the day, but it's not the best (no meal that starts before 9am ever could be). The award for scrummiest meal of the day, nay week, is reserved for the wonder that is the brunch. What other meal lets you sleep in on a Sunday, eat a glorious mix of the best breakfast goodies AND steak, all while drinking cocktails? Brunch, the Domestic Sluts salute you.

Here's a guide to the greatest meal on the planet.

Granola

Makes around 450g/16oz – enough for a week or two.

You will need:

150g/5¼ oz/1¾ cups porridge oats
70g/2½oz mixed seeds (pumpkin, sesame, sunflower)
50g/1¾oz chopped hazelnuts
40ml/1½fl oz/3 tbsp vegetable oil
50ml/1¾fl oz/3½tbsp honey
½ tsp vanilla extract
½ tsp cinnamon
½ tsp ground ginger
150g/5¼oz dried fruits (raisins, cranberries, apricots, cherries)

Making your own granola might sound dangerously close to knitting your own sanitary towels and weaving your own yoghurt, but it makes for a delicious and filling start to the day. Baking a batch for a week takes less than half an hour. While it's only marginally cheaper than buying a box at the supermarket, making your own means you can customize it. Hate raisins? Leave them out. Not keen on hazelnuts? Swap them for peanuts, pecans or almonds. Want it sweeter? Stir in some brown sugar before baking or add dark chocolate chips when it's cooled. Use this as a template for your own dream recipe that will make you want to eat brekky in the morning.

Make it!

- Heat the oven to 150°C/300°F/ Gas Mark 2, and line a large baking tray with greaseproof paper.
- Mix the oats, seeds and nuts in a large bowl.
- Mix the oil, honey, vanilla and spices in a jug and pour over the oat mixture. Stir it through until well combined.
- Spread the granola evenly over your tray. Bake for 20 minutes, stirring occasionally to break it up so it browns evenly. It will still be sticky when you take it out but crisps up as it dries.
- When it's completely cooled, add the coconut and 100–200g/¼–½oz of dried fruit, depending on taste and what you have lying around, and transfer it to an airtight container. It will keep for a month. You can throw in handfuls of leftover nuts and dried fruit to top it up occasionally.
- Serve with milk or yoghurt for breakfast. A handful makes an ideal snack during the day, and if you're feeling particularly virtuous you can even sprinkle it over bananas and Greek yoghurt for dessert.

How do you like your eggs in the morning?

Scrambled

Don't beat the life out of your eggs. A stir with a fork to break them up is all they need. Don't forget salt and pepper. And cream. Cream is very important.

Take it easy when scrambling – the best eggs are cooked slowly over a medium heat. Stir constantly with a wooden spoon for an even scramble, or every now and again for big, luscious curds. They should be creamy, not rubbery, so take the pan off the heat once the eggs are not quite set.

Poached

Keep the water just below boiling – a ferocious bubbling will jiggle your eggs around and ruin the shape. A splash of vinegar can help the whites to stay in shape, but don't add too much or they'll taste disgusting. Make sure you use really fresh eggs; slide them in gently and cook for 3 minutes.

Boiled

To avoid cracking, take the eggs out of the fridge half an hour before using them to let them come to room temperature. There are many different ways to boil an egg, but the simplest is to bring some water to the boil and simmer for 4½ minutes. This will give a set white and a creamy yolk. Don't forget the soldiers.

Fried

Use a non stick pan and make sure the oil's piping hot before gently breaking the eggs in. Baste the tops of the eggs with the hot oil if you like them sunny side up. If you prefer your eggs over easy, it's a bit more tricky but comes with practice. Flip the eggs gently and fry for a few seconds on the yolk side. Gently scoop them onto your plate with a spatula.

Gypsy eggs

This is a fantastic brunch dish. Light enough to stomach after a messy night out, but filling enough to keep you going until tea-time, especially if you pair it with sautéed potatoes or crusty bread. It's simply eggs baked in a spicy tomato sauce, usually with prosciutto and chorizo. It's a great dish for using up anything you've got left, and you can season it with whatever you fancy. Try this vegetarian version if you don't eat meat. Without chorizo, there's no paprika-rich fat to cook the rest of the ingredients in, so be generous with the olive oil and spices.

Serves 2

You will need:

1 tbsp olive oil
½ tsp cumin seeds
1 red onion, chopped
2 garlic cloves, crushed
1 chilli, finely chopped
400g/14oz tin of chopped tomatoes
200ml/7fl oz/1 cup vegetable stock
1 tsp paprika
4 medium eggs
handful of parsley leaves, chopped

Make it!

• In a large pan, fry the cumin, onion, garlic and chilli in the oil over a medium heat until the onion is soft.
• Add the tinned tomatoes, vegetable stock and paprika and simmer until the sauce thickens up and becomes slightly jam-like.
• Make four dents in the mixture and carefully break the eggs into them. Put the lid on and cook on a very low heat for 5–7 minutes until the eggs are just set. Don't have a large lidded saucepan? Then transfer the sauce into an ovenproof dish, add the eggs and cook in the oven at 180°C/350°F/Gas Mark 4 for 10 minutes. Scatter over the chopped parsley and scoop out onto toasted muffins.

Our milkshake brings all the boys to the yard

Milkshakes are fabulous at brunch (not smoothies, though, they're wholesome and healthy and it's the weekend – go away with your five-a-day). This banana and vanilla number is thick and gloopy. Add what you like to it – chocolate sauce, brandy, ice cream sprinkles, even cornflakes to go with the breakfast theme.

Make it!

• Mush up the bananas with a fork and add to a blender with the milk and ice cream. If you're adding anything extra, add it now. Scrape the seeds out of half the vanilla pod, pop them in the blender and whizz up until smooth. Pour into a glass, with whatever bells and whistles you fancy on top.

You'll need (for each milkshake):

2 bananas
250ml/8¾fl oz/1 cup semi-skimmed milk
2 scoops vanilla ice cream (nothing fancy, the cheap soft-scoop stuff is fine)
½ vanilla pod

SLUTTERY TIP
Want a healthier drink? (Really?) You can replace the ice cream with yoghurt. But don't do that on the weekends.

The meat

Here's the thing no one tells you about brunch. You can have any kind of meat you like. Any. It's like lunch, but you don't have to pretend that soup is a real starter. If you want sausages, get a few of them on. Bacon? Yes please! And steak? You can absolutely have steak. With everything else. You don't have to choose, you just have to choose what to start with.

The sausages: Pricked or unpricked? To grill or fry? Whatever you choose, make sure you get the best sausages you can. That doesn't always mean highest meat content – you want them juicy as well.

Bacon: You need bacon. Choose a sweetcure one and crisp it up, then you can have it with everything on your plate. Ketchup and beans or pancakes and maple syrup – whatever you fancy nibbling on.

Steak: This isn't the time for a huge rib-eye. Instead, think minute steaks to go with your eggs, and mop up that hollandaise.

Perfect pancakes

Want the perfect pancake batter recipe? Use the one we showed you for Toad in the hole (see page 52) – it's the same batter, it's how you cook it and what you put with it that makes all the difference.

Remember that the first pancake ALWAYS goes wrong. Even Delia and Jamie have to sacrifice their first attempt.

Heat a lightly greased frying pan over a medium heat and add a ladle of batter (2–3 tablespoons). Tip the pan from side to side to evenly spread the batter, and allow to cook for 1–2 minutes until the underneath is golden brown. Flip it over with a spatula (or let boys be boys and do fancy tricks with the frying pan), and cook the other side for half a minute. Slide it onto a plate and add whatever you fancy.

For savoury pancakes, add ham and cheese, or some sweet bacon and fried mushrooms. For sweet pancakes, go for the classic lemon and sugar, thickly smeared chocolate spread, or bananas, berries and honey.

Everything else

Still space on your table? Then you need some more goodies.
Pastries and breads of all varieties (oooh crumpets, too), jams
and marmalades. If you really must, add some fresh fruit as well, but only
the good stuff – strawberries, watermelon, kiwi fruit or cherries. Maybe some
of that granola you made earlier in the week.

Get some Portobello mushrooms in the oven with some Cheddar cheese and
herbs for the vegetarians (and greedy meat eaters).

And the ketchup and baked beans? Don't even try to make these yourself.
They one of the very few things that taste better shop-bought. The Domestic
Sluts know when they're beaten.

Now you just need a few cocktails to go with your brunch (pages 135–143).

Food and Drink

A Nice Cuppa and a Sit Down

> "If you are cold, tea will warm you.
> If you are too heated, it will cool you.
> If you are depressed, it will cheer you.
> If you are excited, it will calm you."
>
> – William Gladstone, 1865

> "Tea rocks"
> – Domestic Sluts, 2011

So what is afternoon tea, exactly? The Simpsons famously described brunch (see pages 66–73), another hard-to-define meal, as "not quite breakfast, it's not quite lunch, but it comes with a slice of cantaloupe at the end. You don't get completely what you would at breakfast, but you get a good meal." And so it is with afternoon tea. You don't get what you would at lunch, you get something even better – and, instead of cantaloupe, there are lashings of mini cakes. Served during the food wilderness that is 3–5pm, afternoon tea offers three tiers of mouth-watering bite-sized morsels to choose from.

Forget going to a fancy hotel, unless you've got the patience to wait three months for a table and a spare £50 in your purse. Find a local cafe and take a friend for a leisurely afternoon treat, or bake your favourite things and lay on your own spread at home. Buy a tiered cake stand from a department store or haggle for a vintage one you'll treasure (for our haggling tips, see p.152). Or pop into a secondhand shop and get some mismatched crockery to lay your sweet snacks and savoury bites out on.

You know it's best to start at the bottom and work your way up ...

Bottom layer: Sluttishly savoury

Traditionally, this is where the finger sandwiches reside (mmm ... mini sandwiches). Mix different breads with different fillings – smoked salmon and horseradish, egg and cress, posh ham and fancy cheese. Mini Yorkshire puddings with slices of roast beef, tiny shepherd's pies or king prawn cocktails in shot glasses would make a substantial savoury start.

Middle layer: A nice bit of crumpet

Time for crumpets, pikelets, or a selection of scones (see page 82) – plain, raisin, cheese, apple, chocolate and orange – with jam, honey, marmalade or clotted cream. Some sweet, some savoury. No one knows what order things go in with the middle layer. No one cares, either.

Top layer: Coquettish cakes

Time to use your dessert stomach – you know, the one that lets you eat pudding even when your regular stomach is full. Think miniature chocolate éclairs, fruit tarts, Victoria sponge, individual cheesecakes and diddy French macarons. Things that you really, really like, just littler than normal.

On the side: Time for tea

Try a variety of different teas with your baking. Think of yourself as a tea sommelier, matching drinks with flavours.

English breakfast – kick things off with the unparalleled traditional invigorating brew.

Darjeeling – a fab fresh tea with a regal golden colour. It's probably what the Queen drinks. Out of a souvenir Coronation mug.

Earl Grey – sip a cup of this summery floral tea with your scones.

Lady Grey – Earl Grey's delicate sister comes with a more citrusy flavour.

Green tea – brew it very briefly to avoid any bitterness.

Flowering jasmine tea – watching the bud unfurl adds a magical touch to proceedings (you can say things like proceedings over afternoon tea).

Peppermint – you'll appreciate its digestive qualities at the end of your feast.

Chai cupcakes

Chai-spiced cakes to top off your afternoon tea? *Yes Please.*
These buttercream-adorned delights deserve to be placed on the top
tier of your cake stand. Buttercream is basically two parts icing sugar
to one part butter, so – if you're making more cupcakes – simply increase
those quantities.

Makes 8–10 regular or
16–20 mini cupcakes

You will need:

100ml/3½fl oz/½ cup milk
1 tea bag (standard breakfast tea)
125g/4½oz/1¼ cups self-raising flour
1 tsp baking powder
1 tsp ground ginger
½ tsp ground cardamom
½ tsp freshly grated nutmeg
50g/1¾oz unsalted butter, at room
temperature
125g/4½oz/½ cup caster sugar
2 eggs
1 tsp vanilla extract

For the lemony buttercream:

250g/8¾oz unsalted butter, at room
temperature
500g/17½oz icing sugar
1 tsp vanilla extract
zest of 2 lemons
4 tbsp lemon juice

Make it!

• Preheat the oven to 180°C/350°F/Gas Mark 4. Line a
muffin tin with cupcake cases.
• Gently bring the milk to a simmer in a small saucepan
over a low heat. Add a tea bag, turn the heat off and
steep for just 1 minute. Any longer and all you'll taste
is tea. You want these to complement your cuppa, not
overwhelm it. Remove the tea bag and let the milk cool
completely. Some milk will have evaporated – that's fine.
• Sift the flour, spices and baking powder into a large
bowl and set aside. Cream the sugar and butter in a
separate bowl. You may notice that it looks drier than
usual because there's less butter in this recipe. Slowly
add the eggs and vanilla and beat well. Gradually add the
flour mixture and the milk to the butter mixture. Add
milk until you have a "dropping" consistency – it should
drip off the back of a spoon but shouldn't be runny.
• Fill each case two-thirds full and bake for 15 minutes
or until risen and golden brown. Test to see if they're
done by sticking a toothpick into one – if it comes out
clean, they're ready. Allow to cool.
• For the buttercream, beat the butter for a couple of
minutes, then sieve in the icing sugar and beat together
until pale and fluffy. Stir in the vanilla and juice. Spread
onto your cupcakes, and garnish with lemon zest.

Food and Drink

Sunny honey cookies

Mmm, honey. Who knew something puked up by an insect could be so delicious? This recipe is so easy that once you've opened the jar there's really no excuse not to knock up a batch of these easy cookies.

It is definitely worth buying runny honey for this recipe, just because it's much easier to beat into the mixture. If all you have is the set stuff, a few seconds of gentle heating in the microwave should make it more manageable. Or you could just get a bicep workout and beat it into submission.

Makes 10–12 cookies

You will need:

75g/2¾oz/6 tbsp unsalted butter
75g/2¾oz/⅓ cup caster sugar
4 tbsp honey
100g/3½oz/⅞ cup plain flour
50g/1¾oz/⅓ cup ground almonds
zest of 1 orange
75g/2¾oz/½ cup raisins

Make it!

- Preheat the oven to 180°C/360°F/Gas Mark 4.
- Beat the butter and sugar together until pale and fluffy. Beat in the honey.
- Sift in the flour, then stir in the almonds and orange zest.
- Stir in the raisins.
- Get blobs of mixture in your hands and roll into 12 golf ball-sized balls. Put them on the baking sheets, spaced well apart as the cookies will spread. Squash each ball gently with your fingers so that they form rounds.
- Bake for 10–12 minutes. The cookies should be starting to go golden round the edges but will still be quite soft until they cool, so keep your hands off (if you can) until they've cooled down.

Childhood Food Memories

Aaaah, childhood food. Jelly and ice cream, fish fingers and our first ever foodie experiences. But what are our strongest childhood memories?

Sian: Boiled Sweets! Oh how I loved boiled sweets. Being given 50p and running down to the shop with the grumpy man behind the counter. And then choosing between pineapple cubes and rhubarbs and custards. They'd come in little white bags that would disintegrate in your pockets. I still love a rhubarb and custard.

Sarah: My parents were strict about what we could and couldn't eat; fizzy drinks and sweets were banned. I'd escape their brown rice kedgeree and head to my best friend's house for the best of Eighties' snack food on offer (sorry, mum). Even now, a bad day sends me heading for a six-pack of mini Scotch eggs. I know. The shame.

Frances: I was an extremely fussy eater as a kid and my poor mum's stews were my least favourite. Not being able to leave the table until I'd finished my plate, I'd put a bit in my pocket, a bit in my shoe, a bit under the plate and, shockingly, throw some under the table when my parents' backs were turned. Needless to say, dirty clothes, tablecloth and carpet, but a suspiciously clean plate meant this particular ruse didn't last for long before I was discovered.

Kat: My childhood focused almost entirely around cake. Every morning before school I would read my mother's party cook books and fixate on the marvellous things you could do with fondant icing. When my mum made cake, my brother and I would wait, drooling, until our turn came to lick the whizzers (you must always lick the whizzers). Uncooked cake mixture is still the most delectable treat in the known universe.

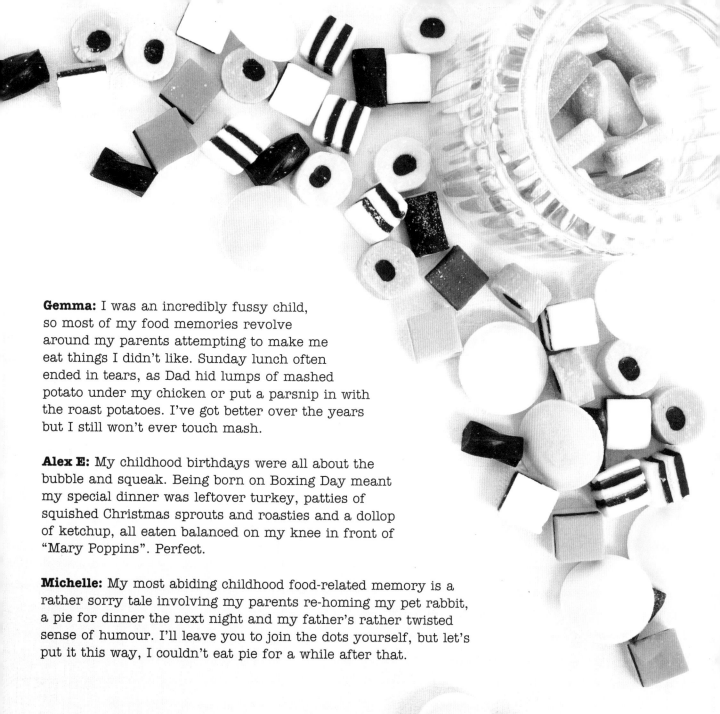

Gemma: I was an incredibly fussy child, so most of my food memories revolve around my parents attempting to make me eat things I didn't like. Sunday lunch often ended in tears, as Dad hid lumps of mashed potato under my chicken or put a parsnip in with the roast potatoes. I've got better over the years but I still won't ever touch mash.

Alex E: My childhood birthdays were all about the bubble and squeak. Being born on Boxing Day meant my special dinner was leftover turkey, patties of squished Christmas sprouts and roasties and a dollop of ketchup, all eaten balanced on my knee in front of "Mary Poppins". Perfect.

Michelle: My most abiding childhood food-related memory is a rather sorry tale involving my parents re-homing my pet rabbit, a pie for dinner the next night and my father's rather twisted sense of humour. I'll leave you to join the dots yourself, but let's put it this way, I couldn't eat pie for a while after that.

Food and Drink

Bollocks to Baking

Alex E says ... I'm a bakeaholic. I think it probably started when I made Victoria sponge cakes with my mum. They were always the same – so comforting. There's still nothing I love better than coming up with something sweet and delicious and sharing it with other people.

Indian spiced scones

This recipe meddles with a quintessential British classic by introducing Indian spices. It might sound odd, but wait until you've filled your kitchen with their spicy scent. Do not put cream anywhere near these savoury beasts. Try adding chopped coriander if you want a splash of colour.

Make it!

• Preheat the oven to 200°C/400°F/Gas Mark 6 and line a baking tray with greaseproof paper.
• Sift the flour, baking powder, garam masala, ground coriander, cumin and salt into a bowl. Rub in the butter until it resembles lumpy breadcrumbs.
• Add the mustard seeds and gradually add milk until it forms a soft but not sticky dough. Scatter in a little more flour if it's too sticky. Don't overwork the dough, or your scones won't be crumbly. Leave it to rest for 5 minutes, and then roll out on a floured surface to about 2cm/¾in thick. Use a plain round cutter to cut out 10 scones. Push the cutter straight down – if you twist it, you'll get an uneven shape that won't rise properly.
• Arrange the scones on the baking tray. Brush the top of each with milk, and bake for 12–15 minutes until well-risen and golden brown. Allow to cool slightly on a wire rack and eat them while they're warm.

Makes 10 standard-sized
or 20 tiny scones

You will need:

250g/9oz/2¼ cups self-
raising flour
1 tsp baking powder
1 tbsp garam masala
1 tsp ground coriander
1 tsp ground cumin
½ tsp salt
60g/2oz/¼ cup butter
1 tsp mustard seeds
150ml/5¼fl oz/½ cup milk

Chocolate cheesecake brownie tart

Some days, you need masses and masses of gooey, sexy chocolate. But there are too many goodies to choose from. So why not squash all of your filthy cravings into a slice of chocolate cheesecake brownie tart (otherwise known as Diabetes Pie)? The brownie mix is a Domestic Sluttery favourite, but this recipe takes it to a whole new level of food porn.

Make it!
- Start with the pastry, as it needs to chill for an hour.
- Sift the icing sugar over the butter, and cream them together. Then sift in the flour and cocoa and mix well.
- Mix the egg yolks and water together in a small bowl to combine.
- Gradually add the egg-yolk mixture to the dough (you may not need it all). If it's too dry, add more water; if too sticky, add more flour.
- Knead gently until it comes together into a slightly sticky dough. Form into a disc and chill for at least an hour before using.
- Once chilled, preheat the oven to 180°C/350°F/Gas Mark 4. Roll the dough out and place it in a greased 20cm/8in tart tin. Press down the edges and trim roughly to fit.
- Line your pastry shell with parchment paper and baking beans (kidney beans and rice could also be used), and "blind bake" for 15 minutes, to stop your pastry going soggy. Then bake for a further 5 minutes with the parchment and beans taken out. Leave to cool while you get on with the filling.

Serves 10

You will need:

For the pastry:
100g/3½oz/1 cup icing sugar
100g/3½oz/1 stick unsalted butter, softened
210g/7½oz/1¾ cups plain flour
40g/1½oz/⅓ cup cocoa powder
2 egg yolks
2 tbsp cold water

For the brownie mix:
55g/2oz dark chocolate
30g/1oz/¼ stick butter, softened
60g/2oz/⅓ cup caster sugar
1 egg
30g/1oz/¼ cup plain flour
1 tsp cocoa powder
½ tsp vanilla extract
pinch of salt
30g/1oz chocolate chips

For the cheesecake topping:
10ml/⅓fl oz egg yolk
60g/2oz ricotta cheese
25g/¾oz/2 tbsp caster sugar
drop of vanilla extract

FOR THE BROWNIE MIX

- Melt the chocolate and butter together and make sure it's completely smooth. Then beat in the sugar and the egg.
- Sift the flour and cocoa powder into the mix.
- Add the salt and vanilla and then the chocolate chips. Make sure everything is all mixed in and smooth. You probably want to eat some.
- Pour your mixture into the pie case.

FOR THE CHEESECAKE

- Start by separating an egg, and then beating the yolk. You need the tiniest dribble of yolk in this mix – perhaps a quarter of the volume.
- Mix with the cheese and sugar and vanilla extract.

TO FINISH

- Splodge on top of the brownie mix and then mix it about and swirl so there's a nice marble pattern.
- Bake your piece for 20–25 minutes until just set. The middle will still be a bit stodgy, but that's the art of a good brownie mix.
- Serve warm, with a side of smugness. You've created happy on a plate.

SLUTTERY TIP
Just fancy the cheesecake brownies? Multiply the brownie recipe by three (and use a whole egg yolk in the cheesecake mix) and bake for 35–40 minutes.

Cosmopolitan cake

Domestic Sluttery has always been known for a love of
cocktails and cake. This is the best of both worlds – boozy,
cakey goodness in a girly shade of pink.

Serves 12

You will need:

For the cake:

225g/8oz/2 sticks butter, at room
temperature
225g/8oz/1¼ cups caster sugar
4 large eggs
zest of two limes (keep the juice for a
cocktail)
zest of one orange
225g/8oz/2 cups self-raising flour
1 tsp baking powder

For the boozy syrup:

100ml/3½fl oz/½ cup water
100g/3½oz/½ cup sugar
1 tbsp triple sec
2 tbsp vodka (if you have citron vodka,
all the better)

For the buttercream icing:

250g/9oz/2 sticks unsalted butter
500g/1¼lb/4⅓ cups icing sugar
150g/5¼oz cranberry sauce
3 tbsp triple sec

Make it!

FOR THE CAKE

- Preheat the oven to 180°C/350°F/Gas Mark 4.
- Cream together the sugar and butter until fluffy.
- Lightly beat the eggs in a separate bowl, then gradually add to the butter mixture, beating well between each addition. If the mixture curdles, stir in a little flour, then continue to add the eggs. Sieve together the flour and baking powder, then fold the zests and flour into the wet ingredients. Pour the mixture into two greased and lined 20cm/8in cake tins (or three 15cm/6in ones). Bake for 30–35 minutes (20–25 minutes if using the smaller-sized tins), or until cooked the whole way through. Cool on a rack.

FOR THE SYRUP

- Mix the sugar and water over a low heat, until the sugar dissolves. Bring to the boil for 5 minutes.
- Leave to cool. Stir in the triple sec and vodka.

FOR THE BUTTERCREAM ICING

- Beat the butter, then sift in the icing sugar and beat the mixture for around 2 minutes until light and fluffy.
- Mix together the cranberry sauce and triple sec.
- Gradually add the triple sec, until you get a spreading consistency. If too runny, add a little more icing sugar.

TO ASSEMBLE

- Once cooled, prick the cake tops all over with a fork. If they have a crust, you could trim this off to let the syrup soak into the cake well. Brush the tops with the syrup, or spoon it over carefully. Let it soak into the cakes for a few minutes before icing.
- Spread the icing over one cake and sandwich the other on top. Ice the top and sides of the cake, and decorate with thin orange slices or paper parasols.

Food and Drink

SLUTTERY CAKE TIPS

Baking is a bit of a science and witchcraft. Sometimes it goes perfectly, other times you're left with rubbish cakes only fit for the bin. Here are the most common baking problems, and how to prevent them from ruining your cakes:

To stop your cake from being lumpy – this is all about the temperature of the butter. Cold butter means a lumpy batter. That means a lumpy cake. Wait until your butter is room temperature before you bake anything.

To stop your cake from falling flat – don't over-beat your batter! This beats the air out and it won't rise. You'll get hard solid cake instead of light and fluffy yumminess.

To stop your cake from sinking – don't sneak a peek. Trust the timings, and clean your oven door so you can see your cake rising in the oven.

To stop your cake from rising too much in the middle – your oven is too hot. All temperatures in recipes should be seen as approximate. Ovens tend to have a mind of their own; turn yours down, tweak and play until you've got it spot on.

Style

> "Style is knowing who you are, what you want to say and not giving a damn."
>
> Gore Vidal

Style and fashion are two very different things. We do love the occasional fashion magazine, but something that's fashionable isn't necessarily stylish. And just because something isn't in fashion, that doesn't mean it's not oozing with style.

How you wear something is always more important than what you wear. In this chapter, we talk about choosing clothes because you love them, getting the best out of what you already own and making a more fabulous version of yourself. Clothes should just be window dressing, highlighting you. Fashion doesn't always do that, but style does. Personal style is one of the very best assets you can have.

Find what works for you instead of what's being plastered across the glossy magazines. Or just slick on a bit of bright red lipstick. Sometimes that's all you need.

THE REAL KEY
WARDROBE PIECES

If you pay attention to "style experts", key wardrobe pieces usually involve these items: a little black dress, statement jewellery and something ground-breaking like a white shirt. Yawn. They're not your key pieces. They're definitely handy to have in your wardrobe, but they're not the pieces that you'll grab on your "what the hell do I wear?" days. You'll stick to your old favourites and they're the items that you want to keep fresh and bang up to date.

THE DRESS YOU STOLE FROM YOUR MUM OK, so she's not impressed that you stole it, but she hasn't worn that dress in years and it's probably never going to fit her again (sorry, mum). She didn't even notice it was gone until you wore it to dinner on Sunday. Want to update this little number? Keep the accessories modern and bright. Try it with something unexpected, even if you think it might clash. And don't get stuck in a black tights/colourful dress combo. Once you're stuck in that little rut, it's very hard to get out of it.

THE SLOUCHY JUMPER First, look at your jumper. Has it seen better days? If it's threadbare and bobbly, it might be time to accept that it's a snuggly jumper for hangovers and Sundays only. Otherwise, wear it with something sexy. Try it over that dress you always feel over-dressed in and turn casual into bombshell.

THE JACKET YOU LIVE IN It doesn't matter what kind of jacket it is, if you love it you might as well forget all others. Try belts cinched around your waist, or brooches on the lapel. Maybe even a brightly coloured shirt creeping out over the top. Otherwise it'll just look like you're grabbing the same jacket on your way out of the house. That might be true, but no one else needs to know that.

THE NECKLACE YOU ONLY SAVE "FOR BEST" The Domestic Sluts don't really believe in saving for best. While the sentiment was adorable at some forgotten time in yesteryear, these days it means that your favourite things get locked away never to be seen again. That's no fun. Obviously don't wear all of your favourite things at once (you'll be too afraid to sit down) but one special item can make even the most sensible of outfits look modern.

YOUR FAVOURITE JEANS You know what? You already rock these. Put the magazine down that tells you that you need to update them, throw on your favourite t-shirt (yes, that Spiderman one you like) and a pair of heels. You're good to go. You know the rule: if it's not broken …

STYLE ICONS

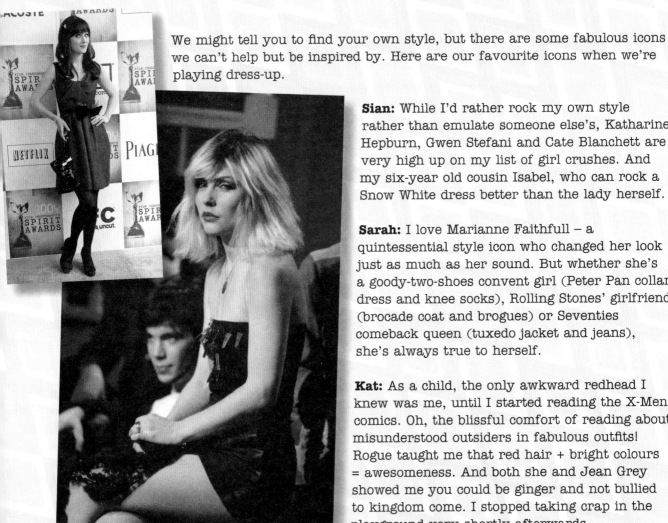

We might tell you to find your own style, but there are some fabulous icons we can't help but be inspired by. Here are our favourite icons when we're playing dress-up.

Sian: While I'd rather rock my own style rather than emulate someone else's, Katharine Hepburn, Gwen Stefani and Cate Blanchett are very high up on my list of girl crushes. And my six-year old cousin Isabel, who can rock a Snow White dress better than the lady herself.

Sarah: I love Marianne Faithfull – a quintessential style icon who changed her look just as much as her sound. But whether she's a goody-two-shoes convent girl (Peter Pan collar dress and knee socks), Rolling Stones' girlfriend (brocade coat and brogues) or Seventies comeback queen (tuxedo jacket and jeans), she's always true to herself.

Kat: As a child, the only awkward redhead I knew was me, until I started reading the X-Men comics. Oh, the blissful comfort of reading about misunderstood outsiders in fabulous outfits! Rogue taught me that red hair + bright colours = awesomeness. And both she and Jean Grey showed me you could be ginger and not bullied to kingdom come. I stopped taking crap in the playground very shortly afterwards.

Sara: Liberace. Here was a man with a diamanté car with matching tool box, spangly baton and collection of feathered capes. He's taught me that if you love something, you should wear it without caring what other people think and be proud to have your own sense of style.

Alex E: Zooey Deschanel is probably the nearest I have to a style icon. A little bit kooky, with a great knack for cute dresses with opaques, Zooey manages to always look dressed up without being either frumpy or trashy.

Jane: Poison Ivy from The Cramps, for her love of animal print, tarnished tiaras, Bettie Page bangs and flashing too much flesh. Also Vivienne Westwood for being so fierce, innovative and original over so many years, and Bonnie Parker for her 1930s gangster's moll glamour.

Michelle: I couldn't identify one single style icon. I have always drawn my inspiration from a number of random and diverse sources. I am pretty much indebted to Christian Dior and his iconic New Look and have over the years drawn greatly from Madonna circa 'Desperately Seeking Susan', and even the band Strawberry Switchblade.

Frances: My favourite musicians have always influenced my style, starting in my formative years with the Britpop era when Pulp inspired me to visit both the charity shop and the library, and Kenickie encouraged me to have fun with glitter. My all-time icon is Debbie Harry. Though I'll never be a platinum blonde, whether in Breton top and converse trainers, or a "Heart of Glass" disco-style minidress, Debbie proves everything looks better with a little rock'n'roll attitude.

VINTAGE CLOTHES TO SUIT YOUR SHAPE

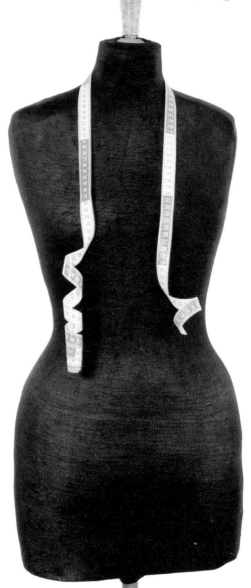

Sarah says ... Initially, my vintage shopping trips were disastrous. There was skin-tight polyester, purple suede platform boots and sequins (hey, it was the Nineties), but after almost two decades scouring charity shops, jumble sales, flea markets and boutiques, and then two years working as a buyer for a vintage clothes shop, I finally learnt what suits my figure. And with so much accessible vintage these days, it's much easier than it was ten years ago.

Vintage can be for anyone. Not every piece of course (I've resigned myself to never carrying off those gorgeous flapper dresses), but every era can suit you – if you know what to pick. Whether your dream dress is from the high street or sixty years old, you're never going to feel at your best if it isn't comfortable and you don't think it flatters you. This chapter covers each decade, describing the look and what body shape it tends to suit. It also highlights items from that era that you'll be able to find easily, so you'll be decked out in flattering vintage in no time.

Key things to know about vintage

• Know your measurements (see page 164). Body sizes have been elongated by decades of huge meals, and a Sixties size 12 is rarely a modern size 12 (this is why you should be suspicious of that old "Marilyn Monroe was a size 16" chestnut). It's worth measuring your chest, waist and hips so you can easily assess whether something will fit, especially if you're buying online.

• Remember, clothes can always be taken in but rarely taken out. Don't buy something hoping you'll squeeze into it.

• The "touch test" can help you sort true vintage from the annoying phrase "vintage-style". Certain fabrics and shapes fit different eras; dresses may be labelled as Fifties, but if they have an elasticated waist, they're more likely to be Eighties.

• Good secondhand shoes above a size 5 are hard to find. If you see some you love, grab them. It doesn't happen very often.

• Mix and matching modern and vintage is best. Nobody wants to look as though they're on the way to a fancy dress party. Head-to-toe vintage isn't an easy look to carry off. Less is more, ladies.

Edwardian

Even though it was over a hundred years ago, Edwardian clothing is, surprisingly, not that hard to find and often in great condition. The first ten years of the twentieth century were a fussy, frilly time with an hourglass silhouette of neat waist, big bum and bigger shoulders. Think feminine silks and lace, which contrast nicely with modern clothes.

DOCTOR'S BAG – These sturdy leather or skin (like alligator or crocodile) bags are for those who like to carry around everything but the kitchen sink with them.

COTTON BLOUSE – Creamy high-neck cotton blouses are often festooned with lace and tons of pearly buttons. They look great with jeans but, due to their often very small size, work best on those with long, dainty necks and slim upper bodies. Warning: these are high-maintenance and require proper laundering, so watch it with the red wine!

LEATHER GLOVES – The neat, white leather gloves you can find in certain vintage stores are so sweet and ladylike, although you might find they're too small for modern mitts. Even slimline elbow-length leather gloves aren't very hard to find, although they might be a bit much down the bus stop of a Monday morning.

1920s

In a reaction to the girlie decades that went before, the Twenties were all about a boyish silhouette; neat hair, small shoulders, a flat chest and narrow hips. The cut of Twenties clothes mean they work better when they skim rather than cling, but luckily for curvier types, there are plenty of accessories (sequins, sparkles, bug brooches and chunky jewellery) out there to let us add some flapper to our look.

KIMONOS – The Orient was a big influence on Twenties designers, and you can still find beautiful silk kimonos in most vintage shops. They're great for glamorous lounging at home and suit every body shape, although they look especially ace on more mature ladies and those with grey hair. Think they look too flamboyant for the daytime? Try a short cotton kimono over your favourite jeans.

FLAPPER DRESS – The quintessential Twenties piece is hard to find in pristine condition (those flappers liked to dance 'til they ruined their frocks) and often shockingly pricey. Petite and slim girls look great in these straight cuts, though, and they're great for skimming your tummy if you're not too booby. Beware if you carry your wobbly bits around your thighs and middle – that dropped waist won't do you any favours.

BEADED EVENING BAGS – These cute evening bags come in many forms: beaded, tapestry, with tortoiseshell clasps or a short gold chain. Of course, in the Twenties you could slip out of the house with just your powder compact and perhaps some cash, whereas leaving the room without fifty-seven things seems wrong these days. Love this look? You'll have to learn to travel light.

1930s

The era of the screwball comedy (rent 'Bringing Up Baby' immediately, for Katharine Hepburn being ballsy and looking wonderful) inspired both cool androgyny and serious Hollywood glamour. So take your pick from mannish tailoring and slinky, bias-cut (and completely unforgiving) satin sheath dresses.

BLOUSES – Both feminine and practical, the blouse was the staple of the Thirties wardrobe, and luckily they suit nearly every body shape. Tuck your blouse into a pencil skirt if you have a smaller waist, or wear it loose over some jeans if you're not so keen on your tummy. Crêpe and silk are the most common fabrics (crêpe's more forgiving and easier to look after), and they often come with puff sleeves or cute details like pussy bows at the neck.

TWEED TROUSERS – This is the decade when us women started wearing trousers, and they were often rather fab wide-legged tweedy numbers. Not great for the very short, but they do work on both curvier and skinnier types. Got a great arse? Then these are definitely for you.

HIGH-HEEL BROGUES – These are the perfect combination of boy and girl or library prude and femme fatale. The chunky heel combined with lacing yourself in make them very comfortable, and they work with any figure and most outfits. Swoon.

1940s

The Forties neatly splits into two halves: wartime austerity and post-wartime austerity. In hard times, clothes get worn-out, so vintage pickings can sometimes be slim. Expect plenty of homemade clothes and neat, feminine silhouettes. Slim-hipped ladies, this is your time. Those with child-bearing hips might want to skip to the Fifties.

TEA DRESS – Although the "tea dress" (something you'd wear to eat afternoon tea) has been around since Victorian times, it's also quintessentially Forties. They come in a ridiculous array of varieties – often crepe or cotton, with a floral print, buttoning up the front – but most have a simple, flattering shape. Pair with tights and heels for an outfit to suit almost any occasion.

SHORT-SLEEVED JUMPER – Vintage knitwear is one of those areas where you should be careful (in case you accidentally bring a moth home with you), but Forties jumpers are too cute to leave on the rail. These neat sweaters, usually with high necks and puff sleeves, are more wearable than you'd think and often come in pretty colours like lilac or yellow. These look great on those with a film-star-style heaving bosom.

PENCIL SKIRT – Usually it takes time for a design to filter down from the catwalks to the high streets, but Christian Dior's 1947 introduction of the pencil skirt was so popular that it was common office wear by the end of the decade. Both tight and narrow, these will instantly make you feel like a total saucepot.

1950s

If in doubt, cinch it. The waist is the absolute focus of every Fifties look, and this glamorous, girlish decade flatters every woman with curves.

After ration books and hand-me-downs in the Forties, women began to show off again with stiff, starched petticoats worn under full-skirted sundresses, leotards worn with circle skirts and rock'n'roll teenagers experimenting with jeans. Those of you with curves can get in on the act by wearing skinny Fifties jeans (always with a turn-up) with a cute Fifties gingham blouse.

PROM DRESS – Whether it's a frothy party concoction or a floral cotton sundress, the prom dress can make even the most straight-up-and-down type feel like a right girl. The cinched waist and full skirt flatters nearly every body shape and suits most ladies, although is perhaps best on the young. Try different lengths until you find a shape that works for your body.

FITTED JACKET – What to wear over your prom dress in the cold? Only this neat, ladylike jacket that buttons down the front, fits the waist and flares out over the hips. Also great worn with the pencil skirt, this jacket works best with a neat waist and a generous chunk of butt.

CLASP HANDBAG – Those who lack the curves needed to carry off the Fifties look can still give themselves a little "ladylike" with a classic Fifties leather bag. Ah, the satisfying "chk" the heavy clasps give as they click shut! Great for clobbering would-be burglars, muggers and NSIT (Not Safe In Taxis) men.

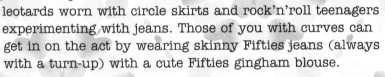

1960s

With its bright colours, modernist shapes and psychedelia, the era of the Velvet Underground and Biba is one of the best for vintage, although it's easy to look like you're going to a fancy dress party at a provincial nightclub called "Time" or "Gas".

It's a decade of dresses and, whether sleeveless, long-sleeved, Peter Pan-collared or empire line, they're all very short. Even the decade's other options (like hotpants) show off a sizeable chunk of thigh. Wear thick black opaque tights (any girl's sartorial best friend) to avoid giving strangers an eyeful.

CHUNKY JEWELLERY – Still comparatively cheap and oh, so cheerful – Sixties chunky jewellery may not be subtle but it can brighten up any outfit. Think long plastic strings of beads in primary colours, op art black-and-white thick bracelets and velvet chokers.

SHIFT DRESS – The classic Sixties shift is a sleeveless minidress in brightly coloured or patterned wool. You might not think the shift, without any emphasis on the waist, would work for girls with large bums, but most shifts are both empire and A-line – so they'll showcase your smaller shoulders and skim their less small bottom half. For those who don't like their arms, pick a long-sleeved A-line minidress.

HEADWEAR – Even though the Sixties was the decade when everyone threw away the obligatory tan tights (bleugh) and gloves, hats stayed – mostly for the reason that some women look great in them. Look out for Twenties-style felt cloches, baker boy caps, sun hats and cute Jackie O pillboxes.

1970s

Layering and brown. That's what Seventies style brings to mind, although it's also the era of disco, flares, riots and the rise of Margaret Thatcher. Phew. The most famous silhouette is long and lean – a floppy hat, maxi dress and platforms – but the increasing diversity of the high street means that anything goes. Which means that there's something Seventies for everyone.

MAXI DRESSES – They may seem like the stuff of style nightmares, but the maxi dress can be flattering and versatile. Depending on your proportions, they can work on both giants and midgets. They'll shows off boobs, skim your tummy and hide your arse. Just be careful with the pattern and fabric; polyester will always cling to the bits you don't want it to.

RIDING BOOTS – One of the most practical vintage purchases, riding boots (flat, knee-high leather black or brown boots) will see you through colder months. There are still enough around to make them quite cheap but leather doesn't give, so these won't work for those with bigger calves.

LEATHER JACKET – Before this decade, leather jackets were worn only by the kind of hot rebels our mums dreamed of dating. But in the Seventies, they went mainstream. Although it's labelled skinny fit, the zip-up slightly tailored style fits girls with waists and hips well. Slim hips but no waist? Then you need a bomber jacket with a ribbed waistband.

1980s

Just because this decade gave us poll tax, shellsuits and A Flock of Seagulls doesn't mean that there isn't good vintage. Think bright primary colours (harking right back to the Sixties), sportswear, Madonna-style crazy layering, powerful shoulders and fun puffball dresses. Just proceed with caution to avoid looking like an East End hipster.

BRIGHT HEELS – Most vintage stores will have at least a few classic Eighties heels: slightly pointy toe, mid-height heel and in a primary coloured leather. Flattering and still comfy.

SKINNY JEANS – Show off excellent pins in some authentic Eighties high-waisted skinnies. The types of skinnies are endless, from ski pants (complete with stirrups) to stonewash, tie-dye and those with zips all the way up the waistband.

TRENCH COAT – Nobody likes those prescriptive lists that try and tell you what classics to own (white shirt? Pah) but in this case alone, a vintage trench coat is rarely ever a bad purchase. They're practical, smart and suit nearly every woman; the tie helps emphasize the waist or create sexy curves where they're needed. Eighties trenches usually come in bright, flattering colours and you can turn the collar up for those "pretend to be a spy" moments.

CLOTHES THAT FIT AND FLATTER

Gemma says ... I've worked in online fashion for years, and in that time I've been lucky enough to interview my favourite designers and attend shows from some of the hottest industry talent. But I'm still very much a high street girl at heart! I've always been about mainstream, accessible style and fashion for the everywoman.

There's nothing wrong with a bit of inspiration, but I'm more interested in what the average woman on the street wants to wear. I've sought to make fashion accessible to everyone, regardless of age, dress size, height or budget.

People think working in fashion is a frivolous, self-involved profession, but they underestimate the difference that a great outfit can make to someone's mood and self-confidence. As a curvy woman, I've often struggled to work out which trends I can really pull off, but I've learned two valuable things: trust your instincts, and don't take fashion too seriously. With a bit of creativity and a dollop of body confidence, anyone can pull together a mood-boosting wardrobe that goes far beyond just boring basics.

The first thing to remember? Clothes aren't about dress size.

So many women struggle to know what clothes will work for their body. It doesn't help that so-called fashion experts teach women to identify their flaws and conceal them, rather than working with the best bits. When did it all get so negative?

Forget your wobbly bits. The old-fashioned concept of dressing for your body shape is what's flawed. Who wants to be described as an apple, pear or (oh God) a brick?! How about treating our body to some nice words instead?

Thick or thin, tall or tiny, half the battle when it comes to finding what clothes work for you is realizing that you're beautiful and your body has some amazing assets. Every body does.

The key to picking clothes that flatter your body is to get to know your body first. Get your clothes off, stand in front of a mirror and pick out the bits you really love. Identify parts about your body that you like and keep doing it until you learn to love the whole lot.

While you're working on that all-important self-acceptance, give your wardrobe an overhaul to help you on your way...

THE TEN COMMANDMENTS OF STYLE

1. Thou shalt start as thou means to go on

Greying cotton undies have NO place in the knicker drawer! Bin them and start afresh with some beautiful, well-fitting undies. To begin with, all women should have at least one frivolous set of overpriced smalls, one perfect piece of shapewear and one nude, seamless set. If you haven't been measured for a bra in the last two years, get re-measured. Your breasts (and posture) will thank you.

2. Thou shalt not listen to thine mother

No offence mums, but when your daughters become adults, you automatically lose the right to judge their outfits. "Are you really going out like that?" is banned from mum vocabulary from now on. If you want to wear an egg-yellow micro minidress with cut-outs at the waist, that is your prerogative.

3. Thou shalt not be dull

Owning some classic and timeless pieces of clothing is one thing, but don't hold on to boring clothes just for the sake of it. By all means, make sure you have the basics in your wardrobe, but don't buy things that are supposedly classics if they make you feel boring, or worse, uncomfortable.

4. Thou shalt own at least one pair of ridiculous shoes

Where would women be without a fabulous pair of over-the-top heels? Every woman needs a pair of shoes that command attention. Good footwear can take an outfit from boring to brilliant. Just remember two things: buy the right size, and check you can walk in them.

5. Thou shalt eventually locate the perfect pair of jeans

Shopping for jeans is a bit like shopping for your school uniform when you were a kid. NO FUN WHATSOEVER. There's nothing like the hunt for a new pair of jeans to make you feel bad about your body. Don't worry if you have to go up a size – if they fit better, you'll look better and love your jeans more.

6. Thou shalt not be scared of tricky trends

Being a fashion victim is not a wise move, but it's also worth remembering that clothes are there to be enjoyed and fashion should be fun. If there's a silly trend that really appeals to you that you want to try – be it a turban, a jumpsuit or a pleated maxi skirt – just try it!

7. Thou shalt not buy it just because it's cheap

If you spend £80 in the sale because everything is "such a bargain", you're still spending £80! So think before you get out the plastic.

8. Know which shops cater for your shape

Irritatingly, although there's a sizing chart for women, there's no standard dress size chart for women's clothing, which means that sizing can vary wildly from shop to shop. In general, brands and stores aimed at younger consumers tend to cut much smaller while those aimed at the more mature lady are more generous, especially around the hips and bust.

9. Thou shalt never slum it

It's one thing to throw on a pair of jogging bottoms and a hoodie and run to the newsagent, but loungewear should be reserved for the odd occasion only. Don't let yourself get into a rut of just throwing on whatever is clean. There's no shame in taking pride in your appearance. Don't be afraid to be overdressed every now and then.

10. Thou shalt trust thine own opinion

All this advice aside, when it comes down to it, YOU are the one who walks into the shop and makes the choice. If you really are unsure what look is right for you, open your wardrobe and pull out the thing you love the most. Use that as the basis of your look and try similar things in similar shapes or colours. Think about what you wear the most and treat yourself to a brand-new version. If you love something, if it fits you properly, and if it makes you happy, wear it with a smile. That's your best accessory.

CARING FOR YOUR CLOBBER

You see the dress on the hanger in the shop and it's love at first sight. A few happy outings later and it's all over. The dress is laying crumpled and wine-damaged in the corner of your bedroom. Everyone feels the guilt when a perfectly good outfit has been ruined. Next time around, just remember there are some easy things you can do to show your clothes a bit of love. It's the very least you can do, seeing as they make you look so fabulous.

Prevention is better than cure

Be honest with yourself. Before you buy, check the label. Will you handwash that woollen? Really? Really, really? If you're ultimately going to end up shoving it into the machine and ruining it, it's not worth it – which is why one of the Domestic Sluts never buys anything that needs ironing. Know your own limits.

It'll come out in the wash

You've decided to buy it. It's come to the time for its first wash. Here's a vital tip that many intelligent women choose to ignore: read the care instructions on the label and work out what those symbols mean. They're there to help you. See our guide on p.165.

When washing coloured clothing for the first time, turn it inside out first. This is one occasion where you don't want to wash those blues away.

The washing machine will make any loose threads looser and existing holes larger, so sort them out before they get anywhere near the machine. A sneaky short-term measure is to use clear nail varnish – that well known favourite for helping with laddered tights – to secure any rogue loose threads on buttons.

Delicate lingerie isn't meant to go in the machine, so don't even be tempted. Think of all the damage that a fearsome piece of underwire could do. You should handwash lingerie, but it's a lot of faffing – so buy a lingerie washing bag and then you're safe to shove your smalls into the machine.

Dry measures

As soon as the machine has finished its job, take your washing out. Don't leave it until you come back from the pub. Yes, it's a boring job, but if you don't do it, your clothes will smell stale (ewww) and it'll be a nightmare to get any creases out. Bonus flatmate points, too, as you won't get accused of hogging the machine.

Try to dry clothes outside on the line, or at least on dryers in your house. Tumble-drying is easy, but it's not so kind on the planet or your clothes.

Heavy knits and lace should be laid out to dry flat, otherwise they'll stretch. You don't want to end up wearing that jumper as a dress.

Linen and viscose should both be ironed while damp to ease the shape back in to the garment. If you're handwashing silk, roll it in a towel to dry it rather than wringing it.

Never-ending storage

Make sure your clothes are clean before putting them away. Stains are better treated while they're still fresh, while moths are attracted to dirtier clothes.

Like hanging your favourite clothes around your room? Make sure they're out of direct sunlight to prevent those lovely bright colours fading.

Get yourself a collection of wooden hangers. The free plastic ones from the shops or, even worse, the wire metal ones you get with your dry-cleaning will stretch your clothes out of shape. Don't hang up your woollens as they'll stretch – they're much better folded.

Don't go hell for leather

Do use those protecting sprays that people always try to flog you in the shoe shop – they actually work. Once in your wardrobe, remember to regularly clean and polish your leather goods – you'll be rewarded for it with years of wear. Plastic ain't so fantastic for storing leather goods; try a cloth bag instead. Replace the heels on your leather shoes before they wear down – it usually costs under a tenner and gives a new lease of life to shoes. Don't stop wearing your strappies when they need re-heeling – you'll soon end up with a cupboard full of broken shoes and nothing to wear on your pretty feet.

Emergency measures

Treat your stains as soon as possible. Don't ever iron a stain – the heat makes the stain even trickier to get out.

Too much singing and dancing in the rain trashed your leather shoes? Best thing to do is stuff them with newspaper and let them dry naturally.

Some timeless tips that still do the trick: try some wax to ease a stuck zip, or add vinegar to the wash in your rinse cycle if your clothes are beginning to look a bit faded.

Bought vintage that stills bears the marks of its previous owner? An application of shampoo can work wonders on a shirt collar stain, while lemon juice or white wine can shift deodorant marks.

And if there's a stubborn stain you just can't get out? Take your favourite shirt to the cleaners right away (no, not in your bra, get dressed first).

THE FIVE-MINUTE FACE
(SO EASY YOU CAN DO IT ON THE TRAIN)

Sometimes an extra ten minutes in bed is far more important than having perfect, polished make-up. Especially if you've stayed out past your bedtime. But leaving the house with at least a bit of make-up on can make you ready to face the day. That doesn't mean hiding beneath a mask of it, though. Unless you're working the full-on burlesque look, caked-on make-up is old-fashioned – a dewy, modern look is definitely the way to go.

With the right tools and five minutes to spare, you can create something simple, modern and natural. Once you've done it a few times, you'll easily be able to recreate almost all of it on the bus or train.

You will need:
• Your favourite moisturizer
• A stick foundation (test in the light when you buy to find the right colour for your skin tone)
• A bronzer compact (with a mirror and brush if possible for on-the-go application)
• The mascara of your choice
• A lip and cheek tint
• Lip balm

Get your face on

Take off last night's make-up if you haven't already. Don't make a habit of leaving your mascara on at night – it's so bad for your skin, and you'll regret it in years to come.

• Prep the skin by smoothing a small amount of moisturizer over your face, massaging in well. Pay attention to any dry areas. Don't skip this step if you have oily skin – all skin needs moisture, and foundation sits better on hydrated skin. Just make sure you buy a suitable oil-free cream. Next, use the stick foundation to even up your skin tone. Use it as sparingly as you can. You could even swap with a tinted moisturizer if you're lucky enough to be blessed with good skin. To hide dark circles, draw an elongated "C" shape from the top of the inner corner of the eye round to the skin under the eye and blend gently with your fingers. Other areas might need a dab of foundation, but only do this if you have to. Letting your own skin breathe is much better!

• Now sweep the biggest, fattest brush you can find in bronzer and apply it to the outer side of the cheek, blending it up to the temples and down towards the nose. Remember, less is more – you want a flush, not a big angry stripe.

• Take the lip and cheek tint and draw a small 2.5 x 2.5cm (1 x 1in) cross shape on the outer edge of apple of the cheek (the fattest bit when you smile). Working quickly before it dries, use your fingers to blend it in really well, pushing the colour out towards the ears, not in towards the nose. Add lip and cheek tint to the lips and blend by rubbing your lips together. The idea is to get quite a natural "just bitten" look, so start with just a couple of drops in the centre of the bottom lip, and add more if you need to. Top with lip balm to stop your lips drying out.

• Finish with mascara. Apply a couple of coats to the top lashes and leave to dry while you do the bottom lashes. Then add one more coat to the top lashes for a bit more drama. Et voilá, this is the finished look! You can add other products depending on time, skill and what you're up to.

The Drunken Accessory Guide

Heading out for a few cocktails? Here's a quick accessory plan so you don't fall over your stilettos and into your gin.

Don't wear your pricey jewels when you're tipsy. You'll lose them and there will be tears before midnight.

False eyelashes a-go-go!

Platform heels are fine, so is the over-the-shoulder handbag.

Planning on having more than three martinis? Then you need your prettiest flats and a cross-body bag.

Wear your highest heels and grab that clutch bag!

You're too tipsy for skyscraper heels. Pop your feet into some kitten heels and grab your favourite satchel.

Pack flats in your bag just in case a few turns into a "few too many".

Nude make-up only! Otherwise it'll end up smeared across your face come midnight.

Think you might end up somewhere in between? Pick a pair of wedges. Just choose your heel height carefully.

Extravagance of accessory

Teetotal　　　　Just a quick one　　　　A few too many　　　　Hic! Hic! Hic!

Amount to drink

LIVING

"If you never did, you should. These things are fun and fun is good."

Dr Seuss

Sometimes the fun parts of our life get pushed to one side (spreadsheets NEVER fit into the fun category and we can't seem to get rid of them no matter how hard we try). Regardless of how busy the Domestic Sluts get, we always do our best to remember to laugh. Usually at ourselves.

This chapter draws in little pieces from everything that you've read in the rest of the book. There are hangover tips to follow on from all those cocktails, and party planning advice so you can show off your baking skills. We'll also share simple travel tips that will make your next holiday the most memorable yet. Just little things and inspiration to make your day brighter and your life a little more exciting. They're not drastic life changes, they're ideas that you can try straight away.

Domestic Sluttery isn't about ignoring the serious, or washing over the bad stuff. It's about making time to really appreciate the good bits and enjoying them when they do come around. If you're lucky, they'll happen at least once a day.

SLUTTERY TRAVELS

Every Domestic Slut needs to get away sometimes. Even if it's just a day trip, time away from home is always good. But travelling can be a stressful, horrible beast. By the time you've factored in packing in a rush (and buying the stuff you forgot at premium airport prices), swarms of stroppy kids on school holidays and a massive row with your best mate, you're frazzled before you've even got to your hotel. Want to make travelling easy and fun? Here's how.

Plotting and planning

Your holiday starts weeks before you set off. Those little places you're dreaming about when you should be working, the pages of the Sunday travel supplement that you tear out – they're all key to your next trip. You're planning your next holiday and you don't even realize you're doing it. Everyone in your office jetting off to the Caribbean? Sounds luscious, but if all you've got in your bookmarks are links to country getaways in the Peak District, book that train.

Glam destinations and palm trees aren't for everyone. If you don't like lying in the sun all day but you're going away with someone who does, find somewhere you can get a beach and a bit of culture. Can't bear flying? Look for exciting places you can get to via ferry. Compromising on a holiday can be a good thing – it'll make you go to destinations you'd never considered before.

What to pack

Packing. Ugh.

Pack the day before. Don't you dare try and do it an hour before you need to be on that train, but pack too soon and you'll only end up unpacking to wear your favourite t-shirt to bed when it's cold. Remember to pick up your favourite dress from the dry-cleaners, buy that new pair of shoes you've had your eye on and make sure you've got all of your favourite smellies in dinky size.

When you pack with time to spare, you pack better. Going away for a week? You only need four or five changes of clothes. Really. Pack the stuff you love, pieces that match and the tops that layer. You'll have more outfits than you realize. Leave bulky hardback books at home, and make sure you've got a couple of cotton tote bags with you rather than a massive handbag. You can throw everything you need in them during the day and a small evening bag will take up less space in your luggage. Don't pack jeans. Wear your most fabulous pair to the airport – they're far too bulky for your suitcase.

Planning on doing A LOT of shopping? Consider packing a smaller suitcase and popping it into a larger one. That way you won't have to cram everything in to one case at the other end and risk breakages. Just check your luggage allowances before you go so you don't get a shock at the other end. And call the bank to tell them you'll be spending abroad, otherwise they'll block your credit cards.

SLUTTERY TIP
Creases like hard edges. Fold your favourite items in sheets of tissue paper and you'll be crease-free, even after the longest journey.

Things you'll definitely need
• Travel-sized bottles (and your favourite scented candle in mini size to remind you of home).
• Sun lotion. Two small bottles before you go will save your pennies and sunburnt shoulders.
• New sunglasses. Just because.
• Magazines. At least three. The trashy ones you love but never get around to reading.
• Mosquito spray. Ouch. Pesky things.

Things to leave behind
• Hairdryer. Even if your hotel doesn't have one, you're on holiday – stop blow-drying and go out and play!
• A giant sun hat. Now is not the time to try and decide if you're a hat person.
• That third swimsuit. You don't need three. Stop it.
• Eight billion pairs of shoes. Which would you save in a fire? Take those with you.
• Work. Your work mobile, your laptop, your notes. No, you CAN'T work on the journey. You're banned. Get yourself to the nearest bookshop.

Where to stay

Want to know our favourite places in the world? Check out our holiday tips.

Sian – Atelier Sul Mare, Sicily. My secret paradise. A hotel and art gallery all in one. Each room is designed by a local artist. They're all incredibly special and so are the beach views. The gorgeous art rooms cost from €35 a night. (www.ateliersulmare.it)

Jane – King Kong Klub, Berlin. A Mecca of monkey business in the dark heart of one of Europe's coolest cities. This is a cheap, kitsch cocktail heaven that looks like the set of a trashy sci-fi B-movie. (www.king-kong-klub.de)

Sarah – Mama Shelter, Paris. The "most romantic city the world" may have been done to death, but this cool, though not pretentious, hotel will help you see a whole different side to Paris. Kooky rooms from €179 per night and the in-house restaurant does the best pizza in town. (www.mamashelter.com)

Michelle – Viva Las Vegas Chapel, Las Vegas. I got hitched here, in a recreation of a 1950s diner. It is a truly magical and crazy place. If you pay a visit, be sure to try a burger and shake at the Burger Joint in the Flamingo. The best I have ever had.

Alex E – Hotel Rex, San Francisco. A tiny literary salon-inspired hotel in the heart of the city. I love the cosy library feel – the walls are crammed with antique books and the decor is much more cosy than clinical. There's a free glass of local wine every evening in the bar. Plus, Maximo, the hotel dog, is the cutest pug in California. (www.jdvhotels.com/hotels/sanfrancisco/rex)

Gail – The Cadillac Hotel, Venice Beach. It's right by the boardwalk and is a good base for exploring Los Angeles. Much cheaper than other hotels in the area. The Art Deco exterior is a little worn, but the rooms are modern and comfortable. (www.thecadillachotel.com)

Sel – The Gershwin Hotel, New York. I've stayed here every time I've been to New York. It's a gorgeous mix of small but cosy rooms, dorms of bunk beds for people on a budget, a home from home for new models and it has an artist in residence. There's art all over the place and various events happening, from book readings to gigs. Dorm beds start from $39 per night with the basic private rooms starting from $129. (www.gershwinhotel.com)

How to travel

Some people love travelling. They enjoy looking at their pile of new books, they like the little drinks trolley passing by, and they even get excited looking out of the train window and seeing sheep. Others spend the entire journey quietly seething at the crying child three seats down. And loathe the people excited by sheep. If you love your quiet, make sure you book a train's quiet carriage if you can.

See your journey as a time to do the things you never get the chance to. Being stuck somewhere on your travels is one of the very few occasions you'll ever get totally uninterrupted time to yourself. Just sit back and enjoy it.

Bagging an upgrade

Being upgraded on a flight or in a hotel isn't as easy as Hollywood romcoms make it look. It's like asking for a bottle of house red in a restaurant and then expecting them to give you their most expensive Merlot just because you asked nicely. Fluttering your eyelashes and flirting doesn't work. Instead, consider any upgrade as a bonus to your trip rather than something you're entitled to.

Dress smartly. No one scruffy-looking ever found themselves in first class without rock-star credentials. If you want a seat in business class, make it look like you belong there. You don't need a tailored suit, but rethink the tracksuit.

Be friendly. To everyone – even the grumpy man on check-in. They have the power.

Go boutique. Book into a cute boutique B&B and each room will be charming. No need to upgrade.

Don't lose your cool. Flight delayed? You're in the same situation as everyone else. Yelling at people won't help. Being polite and helpful will. Mix up at the hotel? Politely ask for compensation, don't demand.

Upgrade on the day. First-class train tickets can cost a small fortune when booked in advance, but if there's space on your train you can get an upgrade for as little as a tenner when you board. Free wifi, tea and coffee and tasty food are all yours for a few extra pounds. Loyalty customers get priority on flight upgrades, too, so signing up for that annoying email newsletter might not be a bad idea after all.

Here comes he bride. If you're not actually on your honeymoon, don't pretend you are. Your fibs aren't fooling anyone. But if you are, you'd be mad not to flaunt it just a little.

Booked and packed and ready to go? Don't forget to send the Domestic Sluts a postcard.

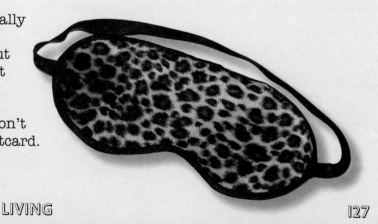

SHOP FOR ANYTHING
ON YOUR LUNCH BREAK

Lunchtime shopping trip. A phrase that gives any Domestic Slut a chill down her spine. You've got an hour, you're limited by the paltry shop selection within walking distance of your office, and you've got a specific occasion to buy for. It's the pressure that makes this difficult. But it can be done if you stop flustering. Follow these steps and you'll even have time to grab lunch.

8am: Make sure you're looking your best. Rushed shopping can't be done with dry-shampooed hair, rubbish shoes and a hungover head. At least start with doing your make-up on the train.

11am: Start your shopping online when your boss isn't looking. Memorize a couple of options (or take print-outs) in case your first choice is sold out. Only choose your favourite shops, and stick to what suits you (see pages 108–9). Don't have any shops near your workplace? Buy online. Next-day delivery and in-store collections are your best friends right now.

11.30am: Start with your favourite shop and only pick two more after that. This isn't a competition to see how many shops you can visit in an hour.

12pm: Ignore that ringing phone and get thee to the shops! (Tell your boss you're going to the bank and imply that you might get stuck in a queue.)

12.05pm: Stop panicking. An hour is a long time in shop world. Stick to what you had your eye on and take your time trying things on.

12.25pm: Found something you love? Buy it immediately and get back to your desk. Tried something on that you're not sure about? Leave it behind.

12.30pm: Next shop. This should be the one where the sale section always has some gems you can't resist. Pick three items in styles you know suit you and one surprise bonus number.

12.45pm: No good? OK, you're going to be late. Let's live with that instead of panicking. Pop into the sandwich shop now. Put in your order and tell them you'll be back in 15 minutes.

12.47pm: Go to your third and final shop. This one is probably pricier than normal but the staff are always helpful. So ask them for help. Put yourself in their hands for the next 15 minutes.

12.59pm: You've found it, haven't you? The perfect item? If not one of these, it'll be the first item you tried on that you're still thinking about. Run back and get it – go on, go!

1.05pm: Sandwich time! Ham salad with extra mayo? Tasty. Leave your dress with the nice girl on reception. Waltzing back late with shopping bags completely ruins your bank story. You're sat in front of your emails with a smile, and your boss hasn't even got back to her desk yet. Nice work.

THE PROCRASTINATING PARTY PLANNER

When it comes to hosting a party or get-together, there is only really one rule: make it easy on yourself! A good hostess can get a party together at a moment's notice (especially if you follow our tips for lazy tidying on page 27). So if you fancy having friends over on a Friday after work, there's really nothing stopping you.

Your main job is to keep your guests happy. After all, you know where the bottle opener is, where the extra glasses are kept for those last-minute arrivals and the dustpan and brush for the inevitable breakages. Guests won't be able to relax and enjoy themselves if their host is running around all evening.

When you've only got an hour

Order pizzas ready for when everyone arrives. Don't forget the vegetarians. Lazy it might be, but no one can resist the smell of takeaway pizza after a drink or three, and they won't even notice that you didn't do the cooking yourself. If you've got a sneaky bit more time, whip up our pizza dough recipe (see page 51).

The hard work should be restricted to before (and unfortunately after) the gathering, regardless of whether it's a massive house party or a few friends over for dinner. The trick is to make it all seem effortless, whether you've been decorating, tidying and baking all day or just hiding magazines and laundry an hour beforehand. By the time your guests arrive, you'll be in your best frock, sipping champers and ready to party the hell out of the evening.

The food

Don't spend the whole night fretting in the kitchen. Your guests won't care about your soufflé rising if they don't get to spend any time with you. Don't prepare any food that needs constant attention.

Serve foods that can either be put in the oven and left alone or stuff that can be prepared well ahead of time. Slow-cooked recipes like casseroles, stew and our maple ham (see page 66) are all perfect. Heavily spiced foods like our DIY curry (see page 42) taste even better when they've been chilled and the spices have had longer to mingle with the other ingredients. Risotto, on the other hand, is a hostess's nightmare. All that stock stirring takes you away from your guests.

How you serve your food obviously depends on the style of party you're going for. At parties, a buffet is the only way to go, but try to do something a bit more exciting than crisps in bowls. Olives, charcuterie and cheese plates, sun-dried tomatoes, pizza bites, stuffed mushrooms, brownies (or our cheesecake brownie tart on pages 86–88) and so on are all good options. Remember to label stuff suitable for veggies, and make sure there are plates, napkins and cutlery available.

The atmosphere

Party decorations are a must. Even if it's only balloons outside the door so people know where the party is, you have to do something to mark the occasion. Not everyone has the time (or funds) to completely make over a room to suit a theme, but fun little additions like customized signs on the bathroom door, posters on the walls, retro bunting or paper chains make all the difference. Pick a fun theme like the 1950s for a 50th birthday, a "childhood heroes" bash or a movie characters party.

Music is always a party minefield, and the sound system will always be hijacked by a friend who turns off your artfully chosen playlist-that-suits-the-theme to put on trashy pop songs. It's best to let them get on with it, get everyone singing along and let everyone have a play. Or think ahead and create a playlist of your friends' favourite songs. That way there will be no complaining.

The entertainment

Big house parties need little else other than food, choons and booze, all of which can be organized within the hour. Organized fun at big events is always naff and you'll find people drifting off pretty quickly unless said entertainment involves someone taking their clothes off (let's not go down that route). The only thing you must do is take photos of everyone. This is for two reasons: the first is to remind yourself how much fun it was once your hangover has subsided. The second is to embarrass people on the Internet the day after.

You really don't need anything more than good conversation, a drink and some lovely people.

When you've only got an hour

Winter? Mull some wine, and fill the house with yummy smells. Summer? A garden party with picnic blankets and pitchers of cocktails will take just minutes to set up. Starting to rain? Have an indoor picnic.

Top party tips

• Disguise cheap bubbly (and make it go further) by trying a simple Bellini recipe. Buy ready-made peach juice and fill champagne flutes with an inch or so ready for when guests arrive. Then just top up with fizz from the fridge just before serving. They'll never know it's cheap bubbly.

• Chic parties are great, but never underestimate a bit of tacky fun. Get everyone in last-minute fancy dress. Even if the theme is silly hats or face paints, people will have fun.

• Intricate cocktails work well for small gatherings, but if you're expecting more than five people, you'll soon get bored of muddling and shaking. Serve wine and beer, alongside a pitcher of sangria.

• Having a small gathering of people who've not met before? Avoid awkward silences by playing games. Charades is more fun than you'd think after a few drinks, but video game tournaments and karaoke can all break the ice and have people chatting into the night.

• When guests won't leave? You have two options: put your pyjamas on, or hide the booze. Both will get them out the door. Note down the number of a reliable local cab company before people arrive so when they start asking, you don't have to hunt one down.

When you've only got an hour

Ask everyone to bring their favourite board game. Your entertainment is sorted and all you had to do was clear a table. Spin the Bottle and Truth or Dare DO NOT COUNT as entertainment. There will be tears.

COCKTAIL HOUR

Cocktail-making shouldn't be complicated, but there's an awful lot of stuff to think about, isn't there? Implements that you just have to buy that serve no other purpose, drinks that you'll never ever drink on their own (Benedictine on the rocks, anyone?), and too many garnishes to choose from. But if you've ever had a hankering for a gin martini and it's pouring down with rain outside, you'll know that a glass of wine just doesn't cut it. Once you stick to a few easy rules, you'll be shaking away like Tom Cruise in no time. Buy the best ingredients you can afford, and keep them simple.

Glassware

Look for glasses in markets and charity shops. You'll find mock '70s Babycham ones for a few pounds (and the real thing if you spend a bit more) and pretty wine glasses in abundance (long stems for white, short for red). Vintage martini glasses are harder to find, so if you see some you like, snap them up. Old Fashioned glasses are short and heavy, and named after the Old Fashioned cocktail. If you prefer longer drinks, pick up some hi-balls. Don't forget the champagne flutes – bubbly doesn't taste better out of a teacup, despite what "speakeasy" bars try to tell you. NEVER put your glasses in the dishwasher.

Cocktail essentials

Gin, rum, vodka and whisky are your key spirits and you'll use them more than any others. But buy the ones you love, too. Melon liqueur may not feature in many traditional drinks, but if you like it, who's going to argue?

WHISKY

Whisky Sour

This cocktail is warm and comforting.

You will need:
25ml/¾fl oz whisky
25ml/¾fl oz lemon juice
25ml/¾fl oz sugar syrup
ice
lemon rind

Shake it!

Shake the ingredients in a cocktail shaker with the ice, then strain and pour into an Old Fashioned glass.

SLUTTERY TIP
How to make sugar syrup:
Add two parts sugar to one part boiling water, then, once the sugar has dissolved, take off the heat. Allow to cool and bottle until you're ready to use.

GIN

Gin-drinking buddies and those who like their herbs and berries will like these ...

The French 75

A classy gin drink, with the power to give you a weekend-ruining headache.

Shake it!

Pop your cherry at the bottom of a champagne flute. In a cocktail shaker, shake together the gin, lemon and sugar with ice. Strain into the glass and top up with the champagne.

You will need:
50ml/1¾fl oz gin
30ml/1fl oz lemon juice
champagne
½ tsp icing sugar
(or caster sugar
at a push)
ice
cherry to garnish

You will need:
50ml/1¾fl oz gin
10ml/⅓fl oz
creme de mure
(blackberry
liqueur)
juice of half a
lemon
10ml/⅓fl oz sugar
syrup
crushed ice
blackberries

The Bramble

This drink uses berries to complement the flavours in the gin.

Shake it!

Fill an Old Fashioned glass with crushed ice. Pour in the gin, lemon juice and sugar syrup. Stir and add more crushed ice if you need to. Then lace with the creme de mure and garnish with the blackberries.

SLUTTERY TIP
Always have tonic in the
house, so when you can't
be bothered with stirring
and shaking, you can
always whip up a decent
gin 'n' tonic at the end of
the day.

COINTREAU

Confused by all the liqueurs available? Cointreau is your best friend. Mimosas, cosmopolitans, lemon drop martinis can all be made with that strange bottle of orange liqueur that you've been ignoring since Christmas. Soon it'll be the most used bottle in your drinks cupboard. We even use it in our Cosmopolitan cake (see page 87).

The Sidecar

You will need:
35ml/1¼fl oz Cointreau
25ml/¾fl oz triple sec
lemon juice
ice

Shake it!
Shake everything up with some ice and pour into a sugar-rimmed glass. It's probably best enjoyed whilst lounging in a giant leather sofa. Or the Ritz in Paris, where it was apparently invented.

PARTY SPIRITS
You'll invariably end up with the following spirits after a party, whether you want them or not: Vermouth (good for cooking), tequila (good for shots, and mixed with lime juice and triple sec to make margaritas), ginger wine (use it in everything when you have a cold) and cheap wine (use in sangria – just mix with brandy and orange juice and fresh fruit and leave in the fridge for an hour).

Lemon Drop Martini

Add soda and you'll create a bullfrog. Two cocktails in one!

Shake it!

Throw everything into a cocktail shaker with ice. Shake, shake, shake, shake. Pour into a sugar-rimmed martini glass and garnish with the lemon peel.

You will need:
75ml/2½fl oz vodka
25ml/¾fl oz Cointreau
1 tsp icing sugar (and some to coat rim of glass)
juice of 1 lemon
lemon peel
ice

Cosmopolitan

"Sex and The City" turned it into a cliché, but if it's not too sweet, it's a very tasty classic.

Shake it!

Mix it all up in a cocktail shaker with ice, then pour into a chilled martini glass. Garnish with burnt orange peel.

You will need:
50ml/1¾fl oz vodka
10ml/⅓fl oz Cointreau (NO MORE. Too much and it's all over.)
10ml/⅓fl oz cranberry juice
10ml/⅓fl oz lime juice
ice
orange peel

SLUTTERY TIP

Burning orange peel isn't as tricky as it sounds. Use a ripe orange, and peel about an inch or so of skin. Get as much of the skin as possible, rather than the white pith underneath. Hold a lit match or lighter over your glass and the peel, about an inch over the top. A burst of flames and then you'll be left with a beautiful-smelling tipple. Let the peel float on your drink as the final touch.

RUM

Something tropical and spicy for the rum-lovers ...

The Casablanca

Sweet and unique, this is a perfect summer drink.

Shake it!

In a cocktail shaker, shake everything together with ice. Then pour into a cocktail glass and garnish with the lime and cherries.

You will need:
50ml/1¾fl oz white rum
20ml/¾fl oz cherry liqueur
20ml/¾fl oz Cointreau
20ml/¾fl oz lime juice
ice
cherries
1 slice of lime

You will need:
50ml/1¾fl oz vodka
50ml/1¾fl oz lime juice
ginger beer
ice
lemon and lime slices

VODKA

Moscow Mule

a spicy and refreshing drink

Shake it!

Put the ice into the cocktail shaker. Add the lime and vodka and shake until everything is mixed together. Pour into a tall glass and top up with ginger beer. Garnish with a lemon slice.

A secret bottle of bubbly is always a good plan. And it should never just be saved for celebrations, either. Once you've added a dash of any of these fruit-based tipples – peach juice, Cointreau, orange juice, cassis – you've got yourself a very simple cocktail.

Porn Star Martini

If you're looking for something a bit more special for your bubbles, how about a Porn Star Martini? A fabulously decadent drink, despite the dubious name.

Shake it!
Mix everything apart from the champagne in a cocktail shaker with ice and pour into a martini glass. Garnish with the fresh passion fruit, which will float and bob about in your drink (and should definitely be eaten with a teaspoon after). Fill a shot glass with the champagne. Serve alongside the martini as a chaser.

You will need:
50ml/1¾fl oz vanilla vodka
25ml/¾fl oz passion fruit liqueur
10ml/⅛fl oz passion fruit purée
1 tsp sugar
ice
½ fresh passion fruit
50ml/1¾fl oz champagne

Shirley Temple

Sweet and spicy, and great if you're driving.

For those of you who don't drink, a Shirley Temple is the tipple for you. Made famous by the child star herself, this cocktail was intended to give her an interesting tipple at flashy parties, without getting her tipsy underage.

Shake it!
Pour the ingredients into a highball glass over ice. Stir and garnish with a cherry. You could always add vodka to this if you fancied it with a bit of a kick.

You will need:
50ml/1¾fl oz ginger ale
25ml/¾fl oz sparkling lemon and limeade
dash of grenadine
ice
1 maraschino cherry

THE SEVEN SLUTTERY HANGOVERS

There are good hangovers and bad hangovers. The bad are when you wake up on the bathroom floor and cling to the porcelain goddess for the rest of the day, calling weakly for tea and dry toast and mumbling that you will never, ever drink again. But there are good hangovers, too, where you recline gracefully on the sofa feeling like you've just overcome a bout of flu, gently weeping over reality TV and idly wondering what happened to your other shoe, before bravely facing the outside world just before the shops close to buy some bacon-flavour crisps for dinner. Those hangovers are excellent. But there are seven of the beasts, and at some point, you'll have to fight them all.

1. The Woodpecker: headache
Ibuprofen is your friend. NOT aspirin, as that'll irritate your already irritable stomach and make you feel sick(er). If the ibuprofen hasn't touched it after an hour, take some paracetamol, too. But for goodness sake, read the labels or get a responsible adult to do it for you.

2. The Washing Machine: churning stomach
You're going to throw up. No ...wait ... you'll be OK. NO HOLD ON IT'S COMING – oh, false alarm. Get some fresh air, take some deep breaths and have a mug of peppermint tea and a ginger biscuit.

3. The Jitterbug: the DTs
Shaky hands? Chamomile tea and some mittens to hide your shame from yourself. And don't forget to eat something.

4. The Oh My God What's Happening In My Mouth: dehydration

There's no delicate way to say this: diarrhoea treatment sachets. If you don't have any in the house, get a box from your local chemist while casually mentioning an upcoming backpacking holiday.

5. The Funeral Mourner: endless weeping

Most commonly associated with gin consumption, the sobbing jags that stem from a sense that you will never again know true joy require a cautious approach. Take your tear-stained face to the newsagent to buy one of those true-story magazines and read it in a hot bath. Your brain will be tricked into thinking you're crying over tragic tales like "MY DEAD DAD KEEPS RINGING THE DOORBELL" and "PSYCHIC HORSE FOUND ME LOVE". You will emerge puffy-faced but victorious.

6. The Disco Napper: exhaustion

You woke up seventeen times last night and now your only hope is vitamin C tablets. Buy one that gives you 800 per cent of your recommended daily allowance of vitamin C in one Orange FizzyGood tablet.

7. The Shame Factory: guilt

Something terrible happened, didn't it? Didn't it? A Very Bad Thing? To reassure yourself, be brave and text your friends. Make sure they're the friends who will say "of course not!" even if it did.

What to do when ...

... you get home?

If you've been organized, you'll have left yourself a pint glass with half-water, half-orange juice and a pinch of salt waiting for you in the fridge. If not, wobble into that corner shop that never closes for a bottle of nasty-coloured sports drink. Either one will rehydrate you and help your liver process the booze.

... you realize halfway through the evening that you're already trollied?

Design a simple test to work out whether you've imbibed too much. For example, instead of firmly staying in one place, does the cubicle lock seem to float up and down the wall? Get a bag of peanuts and a pint of water and don't rejoin your friends until you've finished them both. Sit out the next round and don't touch your next alcoholic drink until you can walk in a straight line to the bar. If you can't order a drink without slurring, it's time to call a cab and head for home.

... you wake up?

The practised cocktail drinkers amongst you will have shopped ahead of time, knowing that otherwise you'll wander around the supermarket helplessly piling marzipan, ham, Quavers, tinned pineapple and grapefruit juice into your trolley in the mistaken belief that one will save you. Omnivore? Steak and eggs will make you invincible. Vegetarian? A enormous lump of cheese followed by a ice lolly. Vegan? Bananas and burnt toast is your saviour.

... you're still hungover two days later?

This is known as being over thirty. As yet, neither science nor Domestic Sluttery have a cure for this. On the plus side, you can probably afford a cab home, so at least you won't have to worry about losing your purse, friends or dignity on the last train.

... you realize you're still drunk at work?

Are you surrounded by self-facilitating media nodes? If so, your boss is used to 10 per cent of the workforce being incapacitated by booze. If not, proceed with care and do not answer your phone or attempt to use email. Sit up straight and look efficient (that means a spreadsheet on your screen, not www.DomesticSluttery.com).

... you know nothing except hair of the dog will fix you?

Bloody Mary

Psychologically, you know you can't handle another vodka and tonic, so it's time for the big guns: try a Bloody Mary — all the tomato juice vitamins will soak up those hangover evils.

Shake it!

Shake everything together and pour into a glass over ice. Watch your hangover disappear into the ether. Don't like tomato juice? Then try Fernet Branca. This bitter digestif has been used to treat cholera, so it'll have no trouble sorting out your desiccated husk of a body. Drinking it is like taking a shot of mouthwash, but think of that burning sensation as purification. Mix it with ginger beer if you must. Like coffee or wine, you'll hate it the first time you try it, but it'll have you doing cartwheels down the street in no time. At least until your next hangover.

You will need:
50ml/1¾fl oz vodka
80ml/2¾fl oz
tomato juice
dash of lemon juice
dash of
Worcestershire sauce
2 drops
Tabasco sauce
Salt

SECONDHAND SLUTTERY

What to look out for and what to avoid

Not into a certain Swedish superstore? Thankfully, ladies with style but not the largest of budgets have plenty of options for buying unique and individual items for themselves and their houses. But whether you're hunting for dusty treasures at a trendy flea market, local charity shop, car boot, church jumble sale or secondhand store, there's

a few tried and trusted ways to find the best stuff. The best thrifters don't have some magical special "eye" that they inherited from their Nan; they do a little research and then get lucky because they shop all the time.

So how can you find the perfect piece that will turn your home from drab to dreamy?

The joy and the pain of secondhand shopping is that there's only one of everything. It's very rare to find the same thing twice (although this has happened to one of the Sluts and completely freaked her out) so if you really love something, buy it because it probably won't be there next week. Not sure? Keep hold of it while you're shopping and ask yourself these five questions:

- Do I love it?
- Is it useful or beautiful?
- Will it fit (in your flat's current style and size-wise, if it's a piece of furniture)?
- Is it in good condition?
- Will I regret it later if I don't buy it?

If it's a "yes" for three or more out of the five, then the gods of vintage are telling you it's OK to buy. Still not sure? Some charity shops and secondhand stores will put things to one side if you ask nicely. If you're thinking about it two hours later, go back and part with your pennies.

As nobody really wants to live in a flat full of useless, cheap impulse-buys, you've got to be realistic. If you're buying big bits of furniture like a sofa or dining table, don't forget to measure the space where it's got to go. And know whether you're the DIY type or not. If you will buy the right fabric, get a staple gun and learn to upholster, then buy that knackered chair.

If it's going to sit in your room accusingly looking at you whenever you're lying around reading gossip mags, then leave it behind.

Things that can be fixed

- Fabric you don't like on a sofa or chair.
- Stains on plastic and silver usually come out.
- Discoloured wood can be stained the colour you want it.

Things that can't be fixed

- Chips in crockery.
- Pictures that look grubby – leave this to the professionals.
- Any hint of moths in knitwear (avoid, AVOID!).

Plan. It sounds nerdy, but a list of perfect purchases will help keep you on the straight and narrow when you're scouring for secondhand. Think pictures torn from magazines, things you loved but didn't win on ebay, books you won't pay full-price for, or even just a scribbled list of items you quite fancy. It might take you a year or even two to find that perfect vintage wall clock, but imagine the thrill when you do. If you're looking for something specific, don't be afraid to ask, because car-booters often have more stock at home. This is also where making friends with the staff at your local secondhand store really pays off; not only could it help you out with sneaky discount, but they will keep an eye out on your behalf if they like you.

Here are some essentials that you should never be without when you're hitting the jumbles (and make sure you read our piece on haggling on pages 152–3 to save some pennies, too):

- A big bag – keep the business cards of stores you love.

- Tape measure – to see if clothes/furniture will fit you/your pad.

- A mixture of coins and notes. Huge notes won't endear you to stall holders!

- Thick tights – often jumble sales and flea markets don't have changing rooms, so these will stop you from flashing your pants in public when you're trying on that '60s skirt.

As the saying goes, "the early bird catches the worm", and, unfortunately for the sleepyheads among you, it's true. The best stuff goes quickly, which means checking out secondhand shops weekly and hitting the car boots at an ungodly 8am. Can't do it? The sleepy vintage shopper heads online – see the Glossary (pages 166–7) for some Sluttery favourites, or head to the daddy of them all, eBay. eBay is stuffed with so much – from the good, the bad, to the frankly weird – that it can be hard to find the best vintage. It's there, though.

Online top tips

• Saved search is your friend. Set up your wishlist online, and they'll get in touch when anything goes online – which does the work for you.

• Misspellings are a great way to find what you're after. "Channel" is an old favourite for fashion types. You'll find bargains no one else is bidding on.

• Watch out for postage, especially on items such as heavy boots or furniture. Search for items that you can pick up in your local area, like bikes. You've bought something bigger than a bike? Get sweet-talking your partner/parents/anyone who owns a car.

• Don't bid until the last minute, unless you want to see the price escalate before your eyes. Just watch, wait and jump in at the last minute. Or, be sneakier and use an ebay "sniping" tool to do your bidding for you while you're out on the town.

HAGGLING THE SLUTTERY WAY

Having a good old rummage in antique and junk shops can be fun, but expensive once you've caught the bug. Haggling is often expected, but it's not about demanding a lower price, it's about paying the right price. Follow the Domestic Sluttery bartering tips and try to bag yourself a bargain.

• Carry small notes and change. This is key to getting the deal you want. Want to pay £7 for something instead of £9? Never underestimate the power of handing over the right money. And that emergency fiver in your pocket is the difference between you paying £55 and £60 for something.

• Timing is key. Is the shop owner being harassed by someone? Not the right time to pester them. Browse until it's a little quieter. And

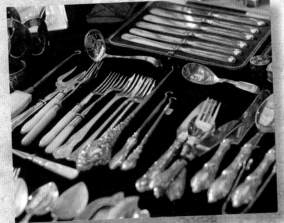

make sure you're talking to the right person. The girl who only works on Saturdays probably can't give you a 20 per cent discount just because you told her you like her shoes.

• Ask yourself why you're haggling. Have a good reason before you start. A stain on a dress, a missing spoon in a cutlery set … these are things that you should get money off for. Buy two or three things and ask for a joint price, or request to pay less for taking it away there and then. Give someone a reason to be nice to you. Don't haggle for the sake of it.

• Start a little lower than you want to spend without being offensive. If you want to spend £20 instead of £30, start at £15 instead. The aim is to get to the price you want, rather than rip someone off. It's their business – don't offend them.

• Haggling is fun, but it's not about winning. When you realize you're arguing over 30p, you're doing it for the sake of it not because you want to save the money. It's easy to get caught up in the thrill of it, but that's a step too far and bad bartering etiquette.

• Don't forget to be nice. Would you give a discount to someone grumpy and demanding?

• Bartering isn't just about saving a few pounds. Ask for something extra for free instead of money off – delivery, perhaps.

• Get to know the people in the shop. If you're trying to haggle in a shop you've never been in before, there are boundaries. Don't push your luck – those shop owners won't forget you. But if they like you, they'll be helpful.

• Remember someone's name, recommend them to your friends, and say thank you when someone goes out of their way to help you. That's the most important rule.

Don't forget, sometimes you're just unlucky. You don't always get what you want – don't take it personally. It's OK to leave something behind. But if you love it? Well, you already know what the answer to that is.

OUR BEST BARGAINS

So now we've told you how to bag yourself a little bargain, what are the very best bargains we've found for ourselves?

Sian: My etched Babycham glasses from the 70s. I nabbed them from a London market for £6. I have to stop myself from buying mismatched glassware at every opportunity. They just end up cluttered all over my desk.

Alex E: A beautiful Art Deco wardrobe that I bagged for £18 on eBay. It has a real Narnia feel to it and keeps my winter coats shipshape in style.

Jane: A cartoon Spiderman t-shirt that cost me a mere ten pence at a church hall jumble sale and which, although probably intended for a small child, I still wear it to this day.

Sarah: As a dedicated secondhand shopper, I've found plenty of bargains over the years, but my absolute favourite is my 1930s etched glass mirror I snapped up on eBay. It was a mere £6.

Gemma: Another eBay bargain here! Mine is a handmade dress with an A-line skirt in a watercolour floral print. I paid about £12, and it fits like it was made for me. The shape and style suggests it's from the '50s, and I'm pretty sure the fabric was supposed to be curtains, but I still love it.

Kat: Like any good Slut, I know my way around a charity shop, and the one near my parent's village in Hampshire is particularly good. I bought some beautiful silver candelabras there. In every house I've lived in, they've made dinner parties a sublimely decadent treat. Not bad for £5 each.

Sara: An enormous blue dress from one of London's best vintage clothes shops – Beyond Retro. It was just £26 and I feel like Alice in Wonderland when I wear it. It has a glorious long bow on the back and crinkles in a very satisfying way when I swish around.

Gail: My pristine, vintage Singer sewing machine, which was £25. It can sew through three inches of fabric – should the need ever arise – and it's beautiful to boot.

Michelle: My best ever bargain was a wonderful 1950s display cabinet with glass doors and gold flocked shelves that we picked up from a local charity shop. I got it super-cheap because one of the locks didn't work. All the lock needed was a little bit more persuasion than the charity shop had tried!

LOCAL GEMS

Once upon a time, everyone used to shop in their local shops. Butchers were busy all the time, you knew your greengrocer by name and your fishmonger was so busy you had to get there first thing in the morning to fight with Mrs Evans from down the road for the best fillets for your tea. Then the massive supermarket popped up. Next door to the butchers.

Everyone buys convenience food. Even the Domestic Sluts are partial to the occasional ready meal. But our local shops are closing down. They're struggling against the bland, plastic-packed meat and shiny veg. They're the most important part of a local community and convenience is killing them. If you're lucky enough to have good ones, you should use them.

The local butcher

• Ever spatchcocked a chicken? De-boned a pork loin? A butcher will do this for you (while you're next door buying your veggies for your roast). They'll fillet and prep anything you ask them to. They take out all the difficult stuff that puts you off certain cuts. It's their job.
• Curious about carving? They'll show you how to do it. Just ask them for advice.
• Want to know exactly where something is from? Your butcher knows this (and if they don't, try the one at the top of the street instead). Food means something to us when it's been sourced locally. So much effort goes into good meat, it shouldn't be seen as a convenience food. Don't underestimate local knowledge – it's the difference between an average feed and a memorable dinner.

- Never cooked lamb cutlets or roasted a quail? Your local butcher doesn't just know about chopping and carving, they should understand cooking, too. They know how to get the best flavours from the meat you're buying.

The fishmonger

- Try something new. If you ask someone in a supermarket to recommend something, they'll probably look at you blankly. Your fishmonger will suggest new things, especially if you tell them what you're planning to cook and for how many.
- Ask and you shall receive. If you hate bones and skin and shells, get them removed.
- Keep reading monkfish recipes but can never find any? Ask your fishmonger to get some in especially for you. Stop relying on standard supermarket stock (yawn) and seek out something different.

The greengrocer

- Massive supermarkets mean seasons are forgotten. Seeing strawberries in January shouldn't be the norm. Strawberries out of season taste of nothing. A good greengrocer will only stock the seasonal stuff.
- What's that weird vegetable? Don't forget the ethnic grocery shops.
- You might pay slightly more for your veg. Get over this and enjoy where your money is going. You're paying for something that tastes good and hasn't lost all its flavour after flying around the world to get to you.

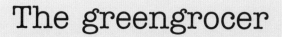

The bookshop

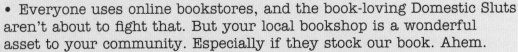

- Everyone uses online bookstores, and the book-loving Domestic Sluts aren't about to fight that. But your local bookshop is a wonderful asset to your community. Especially if they stock our book. Ahem.
- Want literary readings and events? This is where you'll find them. A lot of bookshops have their own book club (some even appearing on the telly), and your favourite author might just pop in for a signing.
- Personal recommendations. Your bookseller knows you. They know you don't care for chick-lit but do love a good historical thriller. Online bookshops pretend to know you, but it's not the same as a bookseller calling you to let you know you should pop in for a new release.
- Want your kids to start reading? A trip to a bookshop where they can pick their own will help them fall in love with books. "The Very Hungry Caterpillar" and anything by Roald Dahl are still read and loved by the Domestic Sluts years into adulthood.

The haberdashery and fabric store

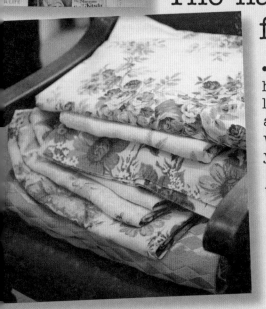

- Got a vague idea of creating a gorgeous frock in your head but not sure where to start? This is where your local haberdashery comes into its own. They'll be able to advise you on the kind of fabric that will work best for what you want to make. Some stores run courses to help you with your dressmaking techniques.
- No more disappointing Internet buys. Obvious, but in the shop you can see the fabric, so you don't have to worry about judging from ill-coloured digital snaps. You can touch, too. You're encouraged to touch!
- Work out what your local area offers that you couldn't get in a department store. An area with a large Asian population is perfect for stunning sari material.

WHEN TO RAID THE PIGGY BANK

Being good with your pennies is commendable. Saving for a rainy day is a Very Good Thing (because rainy days are boring). But there are some things that you should always invest in. Here's how to spend it, the Sluttery way.

Shoes. Hooray! The part of the book where you're encouraged to spend lots of money on shoes. Calm down, this doesn't mean hot-footing it to your nearest Jimmy Choo store and leaving with five pairs of strappy sandals. But it does mean thinking about what you're paying for. Those platform shoes you want to go dancing in? They're full price and still only £15? Your feet are probably going to be crippled ten minutes into wearing them. The "bargain" court shoes you want for work? There's a place for bargain footwear, but if your feet are going to be in cheap shoes for longer than an hour, it's time for a rethink. Once you've bought plasters, a replacement pair of flats in your lunch break and got a taxi home, they're not such a bargain after all. That's before you've even factored in your bad posture and grumpy face.

Home repairs. Don't cut corners here. Just don't. Especially not when it comes to the electrics and plumbing in your home. You need a professional and you need your home to be safe. Saving money isn't ever worth getting hurt over.

Haircuts. If you're lucky enough to have a great local hairdresser who understands your hair and doesn't charge through the nose for a trim, don't ever leave them. But anywhere that charges much less than the norm for a cut and colour should be eyed with suspicion. Get recommendations from friends (whose hair you like) and don't forget that a consultation should be free. If your potential new snipper doesn't fill you with warm and fuzzy feelings in a consultation, they never will. Time to go elsewhere, otherwise you'll wind up in a more expensive salon paying to have mistakes fixed.

Underwear. If you're not wearing the best undercrackers you can afford, you're really not giving the rest of your outfit a chance to shine. Get measured properly for a bra (that bit should be free), and avoid cheap padding, bad underwire and flimsy straps that are going to become misshapen after a few washes and give you no support at all. Don't underestimate your underwear and how it can transform your whole outfit.

The things you love. Got a penchant for a particular brand of tea? Big fan of that fancy cereal with the chocolate pieces in? Spend a lot of time painting your nails with different-colour polishes? Don't scrimp on these. They're the things that make you happy. By all means look for the best deals you can find, but if you're cutting back on the things that really make you smile, you'll be smiling less. That's really not worth those extra saved pennies.

When should you save your pennies?

Books. Get yourself down to your local secondhand book shop, start sharing with friends (book club!) or join your local library. You don't have to give up your reading binges just because you're skint.

Things in tins. Once you start cooking with your tastier fruit and veg, you won't notice that those lentils you've bought aren't the fancy ones.

Shampoo. Spend all the money you want on fancy conditioners, but shampoo you can save on. Don't go as far as washing your hair in washing-up liquid (you do have standards after all), but can you really tell the difference between a £15 bottle and a £3.99 brand?

Seasonal fashion. Are you really going to wear those wet-look leggings more than once? Don't spend too much on fashionable items that you'll get bored of. Buy them if you want, by all means. Just spend your pounds on pieces that will last and that you know you'll love in years to come. Use your spare pennies on the rest.

Things you never, ever use. Yes, you probably should cleanse and tone as well as moisturize. But if you don't bother, even when you buy the expensive stuff, then stop buying it. Don't wear perfume very often? Stop shelling out for a bottle just because it's pretty. And if you really don't like broccoli, stop trying to convince yourself that you do and buy a cabbage instead.

GLOSSARY

Food

Measurement conversion tables

Measurement systems are like drinks – it's best not to mix them. Choose metric, imperial or cups and stick with it!

Common weights to cups

Ingredient	UK (metric)	UK/US (imperial)	US (volume)
White flour	140g	5oz	1 cup
Caster sugar	200g	7oz	1 cup
Icing sugar	110g	4oz	1 cup
Ground almonds	150g	5¼oz	1 cup
Butter	110g	4oz	½ cup/1 stick

Metric to Imperial

Metric	Imperial	Metric	Imperial
25g	1oz	200g	7oz
55g	2oz	225g	8oz (½ lb)
85g	3oz	250g	9oz
115g	4oz (¼ lb)	280g	10oz
140g	5oz	350g	12oz (¾ lb)
175g	6oz	450g	16oz (1 lb)

Oven temperatures

Gas	Electric (Celsius)	Electric (Fahrenheit)
1	130	275
2	150	300
3	165	325
4	180	350
5	190	375
6	200	400
7	220	425
8	230	450
9	240	475
10	260	500

Roasting meat

Wondering how long to roast your lamb? Always over-cook your chicken on a Sunday? This guide will help you figure out those roasting times. Please treat all figures and timings as approximate – ovens and meat cuts will vary your cooking times. Do take care when cooking poultry and, if you're really unsure, invest in a meat thermometer to test the middle of your meat.

Cook at 180°C/350°F/Gas Mark 4 for a perfect roast.

Lamb – 30 minutes per 500g/18oz and your lamb will be perfectly pink.

Beef – 30 minutes per 500g/18oz if you like it medium, or 20 minutes per 500g/18oz if you like it medium-rare.

Chicken – 30 minutes for every 500g/18oz. Stuffed? Add another 30 minutes on to the total cooking time.

Turkey – 20 minutes per 500g/18oz; add 10 minutes per kilo for a stuffed bird.

Duck – 20 minutes per 500g/18oz will do the trick.

Pork – 45 minutes per 500g/18oz until the juices run clear.

CLOTHING

Size conversion table

UK	US	EUR	Bust/waist/hips (remember this is standard sizing in inches – it's a rare lady who's exactly standard!)
6	4	34	30/22/33
8	6	36	32/24/35
10	8	38	34/26/37
12	10	40	36/28/39
14	12	42	38/30/41
16	14	44	40/32/43
18	16	46	42/34/45
20	18	50	44/36/47

Shoes

UK	US	EUR
2	4.5	34
3	5.5	35.5
4	6.5	37
5	7.5	38
6	8.5	39
7	9.5	40
8	10.5	42

How to measure yourself

• For your boobs, measure around the fullest part.

• For your waist measurement, choose the narrowest point, but don't let it get too tight – nothing's worse than an item that just about fits, but will pop if you move.

• Where your hip measurement should be taken depends on your personal shape, but measure the widest part.

(So when they say Paris Hilton has size 11 feet, it just means she has a slightly generous 8 – not quite as exciting, eh?)

Label care instructions

Machine wash cold	Machine wash warm	Machine wash hot	Machine wash gentle	Machine wash 30°	Machine wash 40°

Hand wash	Do not wash	Bleach as needed	Do not bleach	Dry clean	Do not dry clean

Dry flat	Drip dry	Line dry

Tumble dry no heat	Tumble dry low heat	Tumble dry medium	Do not tumble dry

Iron on low heat	Iron on medium heat	Iron on high heat	Do not iron

BLOGS

Home Sweet Home

Poppytalk – www.poppytalk.blogspot.com
A wonderful collection of homewares and inspiration.

Bright.Bazaar – www.brightbazaar.blogspot.com
Mr Bright Bazaar is right – beige is boring!

Design Blahg – www.designblahg.com
Because interior design takes itself waaaay too seriously sometimes.

Home Shopping Spy –
www.homeshoppingspy.wordpress.com
Ideal Home Magazine's unique blog is full of quirky finds

Conversation Pieces – www.conversationpieces.co.uk
Pretty, oh so pretty.

Food & Drink

Post-Punk Kitchen – www.theppk.com
A fabulous vegan treasure trove full of seriously good, inventive recipes. Join the forum to share tips and ask questions.

Smitten Kitchen – www.smittenkitchen.com
Browse by season, vegetable or fruit to find simple, unpretentious dinner ideas that avoid expensive or hard-to-find ingredients.

Chocolate and Zucchini – www.chocolateandzucchini.com
Written by a Parisian woman who isn't afraid to tackle new dishes or techniques, this blog focuses on healthy, fresh produce and delicious chocolate and baking.

The Kitchn – www.thekitchn.com
Prepare to lose yourself for hours in The Kitchn's recipes, tours of other people's stylish kitchens and top tips on how to clean your toaster, blanch your greens or teach a friend how to cook.

Serious Eats – www.seriouseats.com
A seriously comprehensive blog with something for you whether you're vegan or a fan of offal, eating on a budget or splashing out, making cocktails or wondering about alcohol-free beer.

Joy the Baker – www.joythebaker.com
Is there a better internet-loving baker? Probably not.

Bitchin Camero – www.bitchincamero.com
One of the most beautiful food blogs on the interwebs. Stunning photography and imaginative recipes.

The Grub Worm – www.thegrubworm.com
Always honest, always entertaining and really, really good savoury recipes.

Style

The Glamourai – www.theglamourai.com
The most stylish girl on the internet.

Wayward Daughter – www.waywarddaughter.com
Classic '60s looks set against a beautiful Edinburgh backdrop.

Simple Village Girl – www.simplevillagegirl.blogspot.com
Classic British style shown amidst the scenic English countryside.

Foxtail and Fern – www.foxtailandfern.com
Beautiful photography and simple vintage styling from student Hannah.

Wish Wish Wish – www.wishwishwish.net
We wish wish wish we had Carrie's wardrobe.

Living

What Katie Does – www.whatkatiedoes.net
Gorgeous design, wonderful London finds.

India Knight's Posterous – indiaknight.posterous.com
The coolest stuff, covering everything from geekery, to pretty dresses.

The Goddess Guide – www.thegoddessguide.com
Our favourite stylish lady.

Matilde Heart Manech –
www.mathildeheartmanech.wordpress.com
Unique posts on everything from craft to design.

OUR LITTLE BLACK BOOK

We might spend our time nosing about for the next exciting thing, but there are some places and services that we keep coming back to. Here are our favourites:

Armstrongs – established in 1840, this Edinburgh store is a vintage treasure trove, selling everything from military uniforms to delicate tea dresses. www.armstrongsvintage.co.uk

Books for Cooks – more cookery books than you can shake a stick at, plus a cafe that makes delicious treats. www.booksforcooks.com

Drink Shop & Do – specializing in cake, cocktails and craft, not to mention their delectable selection of homewares for sale – what's not to love about this North London cafe? www.drinkshopdo.com

Hemswell Antiques Centre – housed in a former RAF base in Lincolnshire, this is Europe's largest antiques centre, stocking every kind of vintage at any kind of price point. Come prepared to rummage. www.hemswell-antiques.com

Hotel Chocolat – incredible luxury chocolate that's great as a gift but even nicer to keep for yourself. Shop online or in one of their UK-wide stores after Christmas or Easter for the best bargains. www.hotelchocolat.co.uk

JOY – beautiful dresses that don't look like they've come off the high street. There are branches dotted all around the country, and you can buy online, too. www.joythestore.com

Labour of Love – brilliantly quirky Islington boutique (and e-shop, for non-Islington dwellers) that stocks clothes, jewellery, music, books and pretty bits'n'pieces from independent designers. www.labour-of-love.co.uk

Lavender/room – like an ultra-glamorous granny's attic, this gorgeous Brighton boutique is full of shoes, jewels and pretty things for your home. www.lavender-room.co.uk

Marky Market – if you're London-based, Mark will run around the meat and fish markets early in the morning, then drop off the best tasty treats your money will buy you at a more reasonable time of day. www.markymarket.com

Mono – relaxed and airy vegetarian cafe with eclectic decor and its own free library. Ideal for indie music fans, it not only has an in-house independent record store, but also regularly hosts live bands and DJs. www.monocafebar.com

The Old School Yard – want to find the Domestic Sluts having a party? They'll be at this chilled-out retro cocktail bar in London. www.theoldschoolyard.com

Pedlars – this online store has *the* best selection of, you know, stuff, from homeware to everything you need for a street party. www.pedlars.co.uk

Retrouvius – reclamation yard and online store with some ace pieces, from fireplaces to tube signs and school desks. www.retrouvius.com/docs/home.php

Star at Night – enjoy the friendly table service at this mixed gay cocktail bar. A welcoming atmosphere and huge selection of cocktails will make this cosy spot one of your regular haunts. www.thestaratnight.com

Sweet Things – the best cupcakery we've tasted, and fabulous customer service, too. Don't live in London? Then they'll send their brownies in the post!

www.sweetthings.biz

Index

Picture Credits

Acknowledgements

We've discovered that while writing books is lots of fun, it also means months of hard work, late nights of recipe testing and sobbing into our Pinot Grigio. We've loved every minute and we're absolutely full of gratitude to everyone who helped us along the way. Nina Sharman and Emily Preece-Morrison, the best editors we could have asked for. Rosamund Saunders, Lara Holmes, Susan Downing, Georgina Hewitt and Julia Halford for making the book look utterly gorgeous. Jamie Fewery, who sent us a life-changing email one rainy afternoon. And everyone else at Anova Publishing, all of them friendly, patient and supportive.

And we've got a few personal thank yous as well...

Sian: The biggest thanks go to Tom Phillips and Chris Applegate. It's no exaggeration when I say that you're reading this book because of them. They (along with Dave Haste) have kept my wine levels at an acceptable level while writing. And a huge thank you to my parents, for... everything, basically.

Frances: I would like to thank my dad who talked to me a lot about container gardening (and now continues to do so at every opportunity), and thank you to my mum for humouring all these chats. Also thank you to Andy who put up with me ignoring him and frantically typing into a computer for hours/days/months on end.

Sara: Thank you to my parents for being awesome. And I'd better thank Matt too, for putting up with my furious writing rages...

Alex: Rik – thanks for the washing up and devotion to cake testing (or eating).

Sarah: My thanks are for those who made me love vintage; my nan's neat 40's suits, my mum's 80's sailor collars worn with furry boots and my friend Helen, for too many funny try-everything-on trips to mention.

Sel: My biggest thanks go to Ray, Emilia and Marianne for fending for themselves whilst I was busy musing on syntax and commas and to my mum for her unwavering encouragement and support.

Gemma: I'd like to thank my family and friends for always remembering to RSVP to my parties, and Charles for never tiring of paella!

And the rest of the fabulous Domestic Sluts – Jane Bradley, Kat Brown, Michelle Duxbury, Alex Sheppard, Abi Sylvester, Robyn Wilder and the incredibly wise Gail Haslam.

And last, but never ever least: The hugest thank you to our fans and readers who support us and make our job the best ever. Because it really is, and we're very lucky indeed.

First published in the United Kingdom in 2011 by
Pavilion Books
Old West London Magistrates Court
10 Southcombe Street
London, W14 0RA

An imprint of Anova Books Company Ltd

Commissioning editor: Nina Sharman
Copy editor: Julia Halford
Designer: Rosamund Saunders
Picture research: Jenny Faithfull and
Emily Preece-Morrison
Home economists: The Domestic Sluts
Stylist: Susan Downing
Recipe photographer: Lara Holmes

ISBN 9781862059269

A CIP catalogue record for this book is available from
the British Library.

10 9 8 7 6 5 4 3 2 1

Reproduction by Mission, Hong Kong
Printed and bound by 1010 Printing International,
China

www.anovabooks.com

R64007